The Courage to Walk in the Darkness

The Courage to Walk in the Darkness

Turn Crisis into Opportunity

SUNG KUN PARK

Translated by Sarah Park

WIPF & STOCK · Eugene, Oregon

THE COURAGE TO WALK IN THE DARKNESS
Turn Crisis into Opportunity

Wipf & Stock
An Imprint of Wipf and Stock Publishers
199 W. 8th Ave., Suite 3
Eugene, OR 97401

www.wipfandstock.com

PAPERBACK ISBN: 979-8-3852-1088-6
HARDCOVER ISBN: 979-8-3852-1089-3
EBOOK ISBN: 979-8-3852-1090-9

04/10/24

Contents

	Preface	vii
1	Walking on the Night Path in the Dark	1
2	In the Middle of Night, the Lamp of God Has Not Gone Out	32
3	A Daystar Rises at Dawn	72
4	In the Morning Silence, Light Shines	102
	Closing Words	139

Preface

Take just one more step when everyone is ready to quit.

The following story is from Joseph M. Marshall's book *Keep Going: The Art of Perseverance*. A Native American chief had a pretty daughter, and three young men proposed to her. In order to select just one, the chief gave them an assignment. It was to climb a high mountain in the back of his village seven times on a cold, raining night. The three young men made efforts to climb the muddy slope in the rain but struggled. By the third time they reached the peak, they were soaked in the mud, and the chilling air penetrated into their bones. By the fifth time, they all were exhausted to the point where they crawled on their knees. But they did not give up and persevered to the top. After the final and seventh trip, they all collapsed on the ground.

It was then that the chief asked them to get up and make one more trip. Two men responded angrily. Their energy was completely spent, and they couldn't even move a finger. Such a request was outrageous to them. However, the third man, although equally exhausted, got himself back up, using the last ounce of his energy in his body. He made just another step, then fell to the ground. The chief selected him as his son-in-law. Why? It is true that all three failed to make another trip. Yet, the chief acknowledged the last man's courage to take another step when everyone wanted to quit.

In our life journeys, the roads are not all easy and flat. At times, they are like rough slopes on a rainy night. In front of a long way ahead with an unclear view, many people may stop and give up. At such a moment, if we can take just one more step, looking unto God, it may transform our paths. God is pleased with our faith and courage.

Consider people of faith from the Bible. They all took one more step of faith, when they faced a limit or an impossible obstacle ahead. Abraham saw shining stars in the night sky, in a tent of despair. Moses took a step forward, in front of the impossible Red Sea. Samuel heard God's voice in the dark hour of his people. David dreamt a future in the midst of a wilderness in Judah. Elijah heard the sound of a roaring rain from a distant, small cloud. Ezekiel saw a vision of the sky opening and a new morning of recovery while the Israelites were mourning. We need this kind of courage, rooted in faith. No matter how dark and hopeless the circumstances are, God will open the sky to a new morning, if we courageously take one more step.

The reality that we deal with is hardly easy. Many of us may have lost jobs due to recession, suffered closing business, or even lost homes. Some may have felt despair after a serious diagnosis or groaned in pain after going through a divorce. The cries of many young men cover the land as they work construction jobs to get by without a dream. To compare to a type of weather, it would be an overcast gloom, and to compare to a time, it would be like a dark night. What hope can we find in this grim reality?

The night for the immigrants may especially be more dark and lonely as they fight for survival on a completely foreign land. Many diasporas wipe their tears in secret, at a fast food chain, in a dusty sewing factory, or at the cashier's register of a mart. If we are unable to whine or scream about our hurts, or if no one will even care about injustices we suffered, how can we sing about hope in such a cold reality?

Nonetheless, we must not give up. Let us take just one more step when everyone else has stopped. Then let us look unto the sky. God will have prepared a shining morning of blessings. Instead of anticipating easing of the circumstances or expecting a storm to stop, we can take courage in faith and take one more step.

Pastor Sung Kun Park
December 2015
Los Angeles

1

Walking on the Night Path in the Dark

²¹ When Jesus had again crossed over by boat to the other side of the lake, a large crowd gathered around him while he was by the lake. ²² Then one of the synagogue leaders, named Jairus, came, and when he saw Jesus, he fell at his feet. ²³ He pleaded earnestly with him, "My little daughter is dying. Please come and put your hands on her so that she will be healed and live." ²⁴ So Jesus went with him.

A large crowd followed and pressed around him. ²⁵ And a woman was there who had been subject to bleeding for twelve years. ²⁶ She had suffered a great deal under the care of many doctors and had spent all she had, yet instead of getting better she grew worse. ²⁷ When she heard about Jesus, she came up behind him in the crowd and touched his cloak, ²⁸ because she thought, "If I just touch his clothes, I will be healed." ²⁹ Immediately her bleeding stopped and she felt in her body that she was freed from her suffering.

³⁰ At once Jesus realized that power had gone out from him. He turned around in the crowd and asked, "Who touched my clothes?"

³¹ "You see the people crowding against you," his disciples answered, "and yet you can ask, 'Who touched me?'"

³² But Jesus kept looking around to see who had done it. ³³ Then the woman, knowing what had happened to her, came and fell at his feet and, trembling with fear, told him the whole truth. ³⁴ He said to her, "Daughter, your faith has healed you. Go in peace and be freed from your suffering."

[35] While Jesus was still speaking, some people came from the house of Jairus, the synagogue leader. "Your daughter is dead," they said. "Why bother the teacher anymore?"

[36] Overhearing[a] what they said, Jesus told him, "Don't be afraid; just believe."

[37] He did not let anyone follow him except Peter, James and John the brother of James. [38] When they came to the home of the synagogue leader, Jesus saw a commotion, with people crying and wailing loudly. [39] He went in and said to them, "Why all this commotion and wailing? The child is not dead but asleep." [40] But they laughed at him.

After he put them all out, he took the child's father and mother and the disciples who were with him, and went in where the child was. [41] He took her by the hand and said to her, "Talitha koum!" (which means "Little girl, I say to you, get up!"). [42] Immediately the girl stood up and began to walk around (she was twelve years old). At this they were completely astonished.

—MARK 5:21–42

LIFE HAS A PAUSE

Michael Thomas was on his way to a business meeting and was driving in a hurry. The traffic light turned red as soon as he was about to enter an intersection. It was rush hour. Thomas was thinking, "When it turns green, I'll make sure to be the first one to jump at the signal." At this moment, his top priority was to get somewhere as fast as he could. But when the traffic light was about to change, he noticed a blind couple at that intersection. The husband was holding a child's hand, and the wife was carrying an infant on her back. They must have mistakenly entered the busy intersection, just when the cars were ready to jump furiously any second. Thomas felt anxious. "This is going to be bad. All the cars will suddenly brake to screeching stops, and the drivers will be mean and angry." Surprisingly, what Thomas expected to happen did not occur. All the cars remained unmoving in unison. No one screamed. As if time had paused for the blind couple and family, it was awfully quiet only at that intersection. Then someone said, "To the right." He was helping the blind couple. Then someone else continued, "Right, right." It became one chorus of many drivers. The family with disability followed the guiding chorus and safely arrived at the other end of the pedestrian road. The drivers all applauded together. Michael Thomas recalled that this was one of the most beautiful moments that he remembered to witness. This heartwarming episode is in the book *101 More Stories to Open the Heart and Rekindle the Spirit.*

We live in the age of "speed." The faster the better; we believe in the merit of speed. Cars, airplanes, internet connection, and mobile phones are all better if they are faster. Customers prefer faster service at restaurants. Recently, a coffee shop named Cielo opened in my town. It means "heaven" in Spanish. This coffee shop immediately took off to become a huge success. The secret was its speedy service. If a customer preorders, he or she can pick up the order without wait, not even one second. Because there's no waiting, they call it heaven coffee.

But is speed really the secret to true success? Is it really better to be faster? Going at too high a speed may wreck our lives sometimes, and racing only with a forward focus may cause us to lose valuable things in life. A plan achieved is not necessarily a life lived with victory. What's more important is the direction with life. The right direction and clear purpose would be more important than running fast. God sometimes places obstacles in our way in order to slow us down and even stop. If our life is at a stop, it's a good time to examine our faith. God blesses us anew through this pause.

Why Jesus Paused

Jesus, too, had stopped on his way for an urgent matter. After Jesus had performed miracles and proclaimed his words in Decapolis, he went to Capernaum by boat. But multitudes of people gathered at Capernaum. They probably heard about him and his works in Decapolis. Among them was a synagogue leader named Jairus.

He managed the synagogue as a leader of the community. The Jews built basilicas in many regions as slaves of Babylon. There were three positions in this basilica or community hall. First, the hazan was an administrator that oversaw the general operations. Second, the rabbi taught the laws. Third, the synagogue leader managed the operations of the synagogue. Thus, the synagogue leader had been publicly acknowledged as a leader of the community. He was a respected figure in the region. Accordingly, he had reputation, power, and authority.

Notice that a synagogue leader of such status had kneeled before Jesus and bowed down. His twelve-year-old daughter was dying of a serious disease. No parent would sit around and do nothing when his or her child is dying. A parent would go the distance and kneel with humility if it could help the child. Because of his sick child, he kneels at Jesus' feet and desperately makes a request. He asked Jesus to come to his home and pray for the daughter. Jesus understood the urgency, so he headed to Jairus's home with his disciples.

There was another group of people besides the disciples who followed Jesus. Suddenly, an unexpected situation unfolded. A woman had come from behind Jesus and touched his robe without permission. She had suffered a chronic illness of hemorrhage for twelve years. This illness was considered unclean at the time. She had tried to be healed, seeing different doctors and trying various medications and methods but to no avail. When she heard that Jesus was passing through her town, she believed that even touching his robe would be enough to cure her illness. With faith, she touched his robe.

Jesus sensed that power went out of his body, then looked around. The NIV bible in English describes this part in more detail: "He turned. . . kept looking around" (Mark 5:30–32). He stopped walking. He came to a full stop. Isn't Jesus the son of God and the creator of the universe with all the glory and power? Yet Jesus stopped. And he asked the woman about her circumstance. After he heard of her courageous faith, he even blessed her.

Although it must have been a fortunate blessing to the woman, how would Jairus have felt, considering his urgent matter? Wouldn't he have felt frustrated and impatient by Jesus' stopping? At that moment, people from his home came and delivered the message of his daughter's death. He might have blamed the woman, and perhaps even Jesus who stopped on the way. Jesus' stopping brought upon the most unfortunate event to Jairus and his family.

When we face a dead end, what should we do? When we have to give up the familiar route of life, due to a physical illness or a special circumstance, what can we do? Why does God make us come to a dead end? If it was God who made us stop, there must be a reason. And the reason is to bless us, not to harm us.

A Blessing to Learn More Precious Things

God stops us to bless us. The blessing in the stop is our chance to learn more precious things. God has a reason to make us stop. We don't get to stop by chance. There are precious things that we need to know and see. Because there was something he deemed important, Jesus stopped. It was the woman with hemorrhage. In his time in Jewish society, women held a very low status. Women were insignificant and didn't even reach citizenship status. Moreover, this woman had a shameful illness. She had been suffering not just a few years but for twelve long years. Her condition prohibited entrance into the holy sanctuary. She probably wasn't able to carry on a normal way of living in that society. She lived an isolated, miserable, and unhappy life. Then Jesus stopped for this woman.

Jesus' values are revealed in this situation. He valued saving lives more than achieving some great milestones or successes. It's his will that there is nothing more urgent and important than saving lives. While he is the big God who created the universe and performed amazing miracles, the same God also stops and pays full attention to "me" who is troubled and sick.

Jesus cares most about loving one soul. In contrast, people in today's world seem to run in the opposite direction. People like to boast to others, so they lean towards advantageous and external achievements. They validate themselves on the basis of goals, achievements, and missions completed. On the outside, they love the fruits, yet in reality, there's no true fruits that Jesus looks for. Jesus wants to touch and heal the hurts that are sitting deep in one's soul. In the world that values mass and shapes, it would be difficult to realize the true value in life. We should pay attention to what makes man truly good and beautiful.

What is precious in life? Does it matter so much how fast we get somewhere, before others do? Would it be a successful life if we lived competitively so as to arrive at the next destination earlier than others? This is a myth. What's really important is that we are able to stop to love others. We should have Jesus' mindset that allows us to stop our busy footsteps to take care of one suffering soul. Jesus would not be pleased with our mechanical, goal-driven ways that help us achieve our own agenda while neglecting relationships. What would Jesus be pleased to see? When we love those whom we get to meet in our life's journey and share genuine fellowships, he would be pleased. When God stops us, he wants us to see more precious things, such as caring and loving our family, friends, and neighbors.

A Blessing that Strengthens Faith

When God stops us in our tracks, he wants to give us an opportunity to strengthen our faith. When Jesus arrived at Jairus's home, the daughter had already passed. It was all over for Jairus. Then Jesus said, "Don't be afraid. Have faith." Jairus must have thought, What use would it be to not fear or worry, after his daughter already died? Jairus might have asked in suspicion, "What does it mean to have faith?" Jesus meant that he should not look at the circumstance. Instead of the miserable predicament of his daughter's death, he was telling him to look towards Jesus.

Jesus' stopping on the way became a test of faith for Jairus. What Jairus was now facing was not what he wanted. Jairus wanted Jesus to heal his daughter in time. But his daughter died instead of being healed. Things went the completely opposite way. In such a situation as this, how can we trust in Jesus? In an undesired place, how can we believe him?

We may be asked the same question. It is in human nature to blame when we are in an unwanted situation. As life throws us into a miserable situation, we quickly tend to be frustrated and complain. At that moment, Jesus asks us, "Can you still trust in me, even when everything is against you, and all your dreams and plans are impossible to reach?" The right response of faith would be that we will always trust in him.

In Jesus' words, fear and faith are in contrast. They have opposite meanings. When we have faith, fear cannot overtake us. When we have fear, we cannot have faith at the same time. In other words, they cannot coexist. In order to live life firmly in faith, we have to choose one. Our fruits in life would be different depending on our choice, whether we would be shaken by circumstance or whether we would always trust in God in all circumstances.

Peter once walked on the turbulent sea. Jesus first walked towards him on the water and asked Peter to get off the boat and do the same. So Peter got off the boat and tried a few steps. Then he was intimidated by the waves. He fell into the sea. Jesus said to him, "You of little faith, why did you doubt?" (Matt 14:31). Jesus wasn't interested in the waves. He doesn't care about their size or speed. No matter how powerful the waves or the wind are, Jesus says that we won't fall into the sea if we have faith. We should not be afraid.

No life is without problems. We all face problems. Additionally they often come out of nowhere. So it's impossible to predict and prepare the solution. When an unexpected problem finds us, the outcome will be different, depending on our perspective. It's not sufficient to use our smarts and pull all our resources. The problem will still remain. We must rely on Jesus with faith because we exist in the spiritual world.

It's only normal that we don't understand God's world. We cannot understand with common sense the Red Sea split or the fallen walls of Jericho. It's outrageous to hear that a boy knocked down a giant with a stone. The unfathomable God's world is the world of words. If we have the same perspective as those without faith, we will never understand the Bible. Only faith will open our eyes of understanding. Thus apostle Paul had said, "For we live by faith, not by sight." (2 Cor 5:7). We would be no different from non-believers if we lived by sight. We stand apart by living by faith. Although we may not grasp the immediate circumstance before our eyes, we can live strong with a trusting heart in God.

Jesus doesn't promise us a life free of troubles. He doesn't guarantee us a life free of fearful happenings. However, he tells us to choose faith, not fear. We can find God's power in someone's faith that rises above empty words or challenging situations to fully rely on God. When God stops us, we should re-examine whether our faith is solid on the rock.

A Blessing to Learn God's Power

When God stops us, he wants to show us he's at work. God is the ultimate solver of any problem or circumstance. To let us know, he stops our way.

As Jesus entered Jairus's home, people were crying in grief. No parent would sit still upon a loved child's death. Their spirits had to have been agitated and despaired. It's only normal that they are sadly crying. Amidst this, someone sneered at Jesus. He criticized that he came too late as it's already over. He was certain that a death couldn't be overturned by anyone.

Jesus shouted, holding the girl's hand, "My child, get up (talitha cumi)." In Aramaic, talitha means "girl" and cumi means "get up." Jesus commanded that the girl rise from death. Immediately, the dead body got up and walked. The connecting word between Jesus' command and the girl's action is "immediately." The girl immediately got up and walked. As soon as Jesus said to her to get up, she did immediately.

Is something being delayed for some unclear reasons? Are you dealing with a problem so tangled up and complex that there's no solution in sight? Are you at a dead end like the death of Jairus's daughter? Even if the situation appears hopeless, Jesus can overturn it. With his touch, you can get up immediately. God himself is at work. When God intervenes, the impossible problems will get resolved his way.

It's a blessing to us when God allows a stop to our lives. When we come to a stop midway, we can look beyond despair and ponder his reason for stopping us. We should not give up or stay beaten. God has a big miracle in store after our stop. We should rely on God and focus on his works instead of relying on our resources, efforts, and strategies. The stops he allows us will reveal his glory.

Do not rely on the circumstance and environment you are in. They change. It may be a breeze today but a rainstorm tomorrow. Do not rely on people, either. They change according to personal gains and profits. You will surely be disappointed someday. But God loves us all the way to the end. He delivers his promises without fail. If we keep on walking with faithful God, he will turn our stops into miracles.

COME AS YOU ARE

[8]"Ephraim mixes with the nations;
  Ephraim is a flat loaf not turned over.
[9] Foreigners sap his strength,
  but he does not realize it.
His hair is sprinkled with gray,
  but he does not notice.
[10] Israel's arrogance testifies against him,
  but despite all this
he does not return to the Lord his God
  or search for him.
[11] "Ephraim is like a dove,
  easily deceived and senseless—
now calling to Egypt,
  now turning to Assyria.
[12] When they go, I will throw my net over them;
  I will pull them down like the birds in the sky.
When I hear them flocking together,
  I will catch them.
[13] Woe to them,
  because they have strayed from me!
Destruction to them,
  because they have rebelled against me!
I long to redeem them

but they speak about me falsely.
¹⁴ They do not cry out to me from their hearts
   but wail on their beds.
They slash themselves,[a] appealing to their gods
   for grain and new wine,
   but they turn away from me.
¹⁵ I trained them and strengthened their arms,
   but they plot evil against me.
¹⁶ They do not turn to the Most High;
   they are like a faulty bow.
Their leaders will fall by the sword
   because of their insolent words.
For this they will be ridiculed
   in the land of Egypt." (Hos 7:8–16)

Let's visit the "Fox and the Grapes" story, one of Aesop's fables. One day a fox saw a vine over the high wall. Grapes were hanging on the vine branches, but he couldn't reach. They were above his height. He attempted many times but failed. Then the fox told his friends, "Those grapes are probably sour anyway." That was a lame excuse to cover his incompetence. In today's world, many people live with the similar attitude. These people justify their failures, saying, "That would've been a disappointment anyway."

A German writer, Erich Kästner, rewrote "The Fox and the Grapes" in a modern version. In his version, the fox finally succeeds at getting the grapes after his numerous efforts. His animal friends all cheer and applaud at his success. But when the fox tastes the grapes, they are indeed sour. Did the fox then complain about the sour taste? Not at all. He pretended to enjoy the fruit, saying "These are the sweetest grapes that I've ever eaten!" He continued to pick and eat the grapes until he died of a stomach ulcer.

Erich Kästner's story seems to point out the false pretense of modern people. They pretend to be happy when they are not. They pretend to own something when they don't. They pretend to be okay when they are hurting in pain. They cover up and self-justify so they feel good and beautiful about themselves. But this is a dangerous act. They may overlook the real selves and be tricked by the false images. It's better to say the grapes are sour. It's better to say life stings. When you confess your pain honestly, the treatment becomes possible. We get an opportunity of recovery when we are honest before God and true to ourselves.

In today's world, even Christians exaggerate themselves and pretend to be better than they are. They brag and advertise that they are holy people of God. A theologian, Dallas Willard, described these in his book *The Divine Conspiracy* as balloon or ad faith. The "ad faith" is loud and flashy like advertisements, yet it is without substance. In a similar vein, Jesus scolded the Israelites, comparing them to a fruitless fig tree. The tree, full of leaves without fruits, seems to mirror the empty pretense of the religious people of this age. God's works cannot transpire with this type of people. If you desire to experience a truly transformed life in God, I urge you to come to God honestly without false pretense.

To Take Off False Clothes

In reality, the heart of the Israelites had left God, despite their outer appearance. As a result, Ephraim mixed with the nations. The northern kingdom, Israel, accepted the gentiles and their cultures into their own. This meant that the Israelites also worshiped other gods and idols.

Hosea compared this behavior of the Israelites to the "flat loaf that is not turned over." It's a flat loaf, similar to the Korean pancake bindaetteok. In Hosea's eyes, Israel is like a loaf that is cooked only on one side. What would happen to a bindaetteok, if we didn't turn it over? The top side may look okay, but the bottom may burn. Hosea was pointing out the spiritual double-sidedness of the Israelites.

Israel's outer appearance is decent. It even appears holy. They honored God, offered sacrifices, and studied the Law. They look like faithful and lively people. However, the reality was that their lives were full of sin and corruptions that the fire of God's judgment may have already started to burn. Had Israel not even known God in the first place, they might have had a chance to come clean. They might have had a chance to repent and come to God as non-believers. But Israel pretended to be godly while their heart was far from God, so their history became even more deserted. For this reason, Hosea points out that Israel didn't realize that the gentiles overtook their power even when they became old with white hair. Israel's own vitality was deteriorating, as they were mixed and influenced by the gentiles' cultures and idols. The "white hair" implies being near the end of a life. Still, Israel doesn't realize their status. They were so corrupted that they couldn't see that the history of their people was at great jeopardy.

Double-sided Israel had left God yet boasted its empty shell. Israel's arrogance was especially revealed on its face. "Arrogance" means false pride. In actuality, there's nothing to brag about, but arrogant people pretend to have something. This kind of empty faith may call on God but doesn't return to him. The outer appearance is holy, but the reality is a state of separation from God.

Next, the disobedient Israelites, much like foolish pigeons lacking wisdom, head to Assyria after crying towards Egypt. They lacked a sense of direction. For Israelites, God prepared judgment. He said that he would punish them by casting the net. Here we find the caveat of empty faith. It ultimately leads to defeat.

We should watch out for empty faith. We should let go of our egotistical desire to brag and the false appearance of godliness. The real possessor doesn't need to pretend. When they lack the essentials, they focus on grooming the outer appearance. The same applies to church. If church keeps the real gospel at center, it doesn't have any reason to boast about its building or the size of its congregation. The common issue with today's church is that it focuses more on its appearance than the gospel and Jesus' cross. We should heed this age that measures the success of church by decent buildings or finance.

Why did the Catholic church of the Middle Ages collapse? The Catholic Church, too, was pure in the beginning. It loved God and adored worshiping him. However, as the Catholic church grew, the world's power and materials started to flow in. The power of the pope started to surpass that of the emperor. As the world began to fill the cathedrals, they started to beautify the buildings. But after the most important element, the gospel, left church, only the empty buildings now remain.

I was shocked after recently reading a newspaper article about a Catholic priest. It said that the Roman Catholic church collapsed due to its compromise with secular influences. It also said that ironically the Protestant church was also following its footsteps. This is a clear red signal, to see the resemblance of the very system the Protestant church had stood up against and sought to reform. God is not fooled by packaging. He doesn't care about our appearance. We may act godly, but he won't be fooled. The church and its members should have the essence, the gospel. We must take off falsehood and be authentic. Only then we can enter the spiritual realm in his blessings. How can we come before God honestly, without any pretense and falsehood?

See Him Face-to-Face Honestly

We need an honest face-to-face in order to shed the outer pretense and come before God. We need this attitude of honesty not only with ourselves but with God. Who would enjoy looking into themselves? Unless you are very narcissistic, it wouldn't be a welcome thing to do. We know our real selves are imperfect and stained. However, unless we face ourselves with complete honesty, we cannot resolve the problems.

When God was about to resolve the Northern Kingdom, Israel's problems, "the sins of Ephraim and the crimes of Samaria" (Hos 7:1) were exposed. Ephraim refers to the ten tribes of the Northern Kingdom, and Samaria is its capital city. Thus, both the sins of Ephraim and the crimes of Samaria mean the sins and crimes of Israel. Interestingly their sins and crimes were covered. Only when God approached to resolve them, they were then revealed. The first step of the cure is to expose the wound. We cannot be cured if we run away or simply cover the pain and embarrassment of our sins when God exposes them. We have to look squarely at our wound even if it's painful and difficult. We need to face our real selves in order to come before God with honesty.

Ezekiel the prophet saw an amazing vision of the fallen Israelites being restored by God and recorded it. He saw in the vision that the fallen troops that looked like dry bones were restored to become God's great army. Notice that there was a designated place that Ezekiel had to be in to see this vision. It was a valley. It wasn't a mere valley but a valley filled with dead bones. To be more exact, they were skeletons. Skeletons are the remains of a dead body after the flesh decays and decomposes to ashes, which then get blown away by wind. Why did God command Ezekiel to pass through the valley of skeletons? Wouldn't it be far better if God just went ahead and restored Israel? But it wasn't how God restored. Although it may bring pain to Ezekiel on a personal level, God required that he pass through the miserable valley of skeleton-like Israel before he restored it.

It's the same way with our lives. After we honestly acknowledge our sins, salvation will be manifested to us. These days people don't want to hear sermons about sin.

It would add more discomfort to their church experience if they heard about the consequences of sin when it's already taxing to come to church. So, many churches tend to give compliments and encouragement to help their regular church attendance. Sunday messages often stay on a positive note, such as sharing how to receive blessings. As a consequence, it's rare to hear sin proclaimed. It's rare to even hear the word "sin." Alternative expressions are used, as they sound better. One main substitute is "wound." While sin (for which we are at fault) gives us no room for compromise, a wound allows us to be victims. We can blame others for our wound, reassuring with a false illusion of exempting from the consequences of our sin. This represents today's mainstream sermons being at jeopardy.

No matter how uninviting, sin is still there. Sin is still sin, even when we package it with other substituting words. Thus, there's no other solution that liquidates sin. We should acknowledge that we are sinners and come before Jesus Christ the Redeemer. We should not expect redemption without the cross. Dishonest faith that covers and hides itself won't be a ticket to redemption and salvation.

Let me share a rather shocking passage from the Gospels. It's about the Pharisees. Although we, the Christians of the modern age, regard them as the typical example of sinners, at the time when they lived, their reputation was quite different. They led a holy movement during the time of Jesus. Their name originates from the Hebrew word "parush," meaning "one who is separated." They were called godly, as they were separated and differentiated from the world. Still, Jesus said to this godly group of people. "Truly I tell you, the tax collectors and the prostitutes are entering the kingdom of God ahead of you" (Matt 21:31). This is outrageous in that period. The Pharisees meditated the Law every day and fasted twice a week. They made sure to help the needy and observed the Sabbath. They went to pray at the sanctuary, raising their hands high to praise the Lord. Yet Jesus said that they were worse off spiritually than the tax collectors or the prostitutes. Don't mistake this as meaning that prostitutes or tax collectors are clean. One may argue that their sins are more and heavier by objective standards. But Jesus wasn't interested in the amount of sin. He cares about honesty before him. The Pharisees and the tax collectors are all the same in that they are sinners before God. Because the tax collectors confessed that they were sinners, they were acknowledged as God's people. On the other hand, in God's point of view, the double-sided Pharisees were not the citizens of heaven.

Let's look squarely at ourselves, although it may be uncomfortable. We have to see our faults. We have to acknowledge our sin and come before Jesus. Only then a transformation occurs. A true healing begins. We must be honest if we want to come to the Lord.

Yearn for God with All of Our Hearts

We also need to yearn fervently in order to come to the Lord. Do not end short by just meeting him. We should cry out with all of our hearts to him. Israel's other problem was that they didn't wholeheartedly cry to the Lord. Israelites called on the Lord. They probably called on him when they were worshiping, praying, or studying the words. But their hearts were not fully in it. The partial faith is fairly dangerous. Incomplete repentance can even worsen our (spiritual) lives. Take an example of a mole on the body. Unless we remove it completely to its root, it may develop to be an infection, a bigger problem. Uprooting it may be more painful, yet it's the right path to complete healing. Likewise, we should repent all the way when it comes to our relationship with God. We should call on God from the deepest part of our heart. God will start to work with us.

However, Israelites didn't repent all the way. They stopped short. Their cry was not whole-hearted, as they cried only at bedside. Why did they cry at bedside? It means that they were mourning their exhausting lives. They were feeling sad for their lives and so called on God to comfort themselves. Israelites also gathered to get grains and new wine. These were to celebrate the joy of the seasons. They were focusing more on honoring their own efforts and enjoying the fruits rather than giving thanks to God for the harvest of their land.

Crying in our beds won't take care of our problems when they appear. The closed door will be opened only by our Savior when we wholeheartedly cry out to him. We should cry out to him, as if this is the only and last chance we get. Heaven opens when we come to the Lord with all of our hearts. Miracles will happen. We will witness and have an unprecedented experience in the domain of his amazing power.

There are times to pray quietly and times to pray fervently with cries. I urge you to yearn for God's presence and cry out to him when you face hopeless dilemma with your family or special situations in life. If you want to see him, pour your heart and seek him.

Return to God

Lastly, we need to return to the Lord Most High in order to remove our empty shells and come before him. Our final destination is the Most High God. The Israelites had returned, but not to the "Most High." Hosea the prophet keeps rebuking them, as their faith is only partial. They didn't seek God all the way, and they returned to somewhere else. They only had a religious appearance. So, a true transformation did not happen.

Israelites should have returned to the "Most High" God. The Hebrew phrase "El Elyon" is God's nickname, meaning "the Most High." Our God is the highest being, and it is only appropriate that we return to his arms. Our God is above all names and governs all the creations in the universe. He can make us alive or dead, rich or poor, or upright or low in stature. We have to return to our God, for when we return to him, we find the solutions of life.

Unfortunately, Israel was heading towards Egypt instead of God. Would Egypt welcome them if God's people came to Egypt? Not likely. Egypt was mocking and laughing at Israel. Let's assume that Christians mingle with non-Christians once in a while, blending in their secular culture. If a pastor were to forget about his or her identity and just drink alcohol to fit in with the rest of the world, would people respect him or her for being so understanding? Not at all. They would laugh at the pastor. They would criticize and question his or her faith as well as qualification as pastor. Jesus said that if salt loses its flavor, people would trample it. Salt keeps its value when it's salty. Likewise, Christians should behave like Christians anywhere. It's not wise to compromise and blend in with the secular culture. As godly people, we should transform the world. Christians are able to find solutions to life's problems when we return to God the Most High, the creator.

Let me refresh. Who is the Most High? Who guides our lives and governs them? Don't let it be the Blue House, the White House, materials, fame, or power. We only have one Lord. I urge you to surrender your life to the El Elyon God and confidently grow the roots of faith.

Let us examine our image before the Lord. Is there still a lingering temptation to look more holy than we actually are? We cannot do a face-to-face with God until we break this temptation. Let us confess our sin that separates us from God and return to him. We don't have to wait until our sin is all forgiven or taken care of. We should come to him as we are now. Then God will receive us as we are and bless us.

This anecdote happened to a famous evangelist, D. L. Moody, after he preached about salvation at a revival. It was time to invite those who newly committed to faith, and a girl walked up to the front down the middle aisle. People noticed her untidy and unclean look and suspected that she didn't take a bath for a while, as she smelled. People guessed that she wasn't being schooled, and she might be an orphan. This poor girl went up to Moody and asked, "Does God love an unlovely, uneducated, and abandoned person like me?" Moody responded to her and confirmed to her right away, "Yes. He will take you as you are." That day, the girl accepted Jesus as her personal Lord and Savior. Elizabeth Hamilton was watching this and was touched. She was inspired to write the lyrics and with David Sankey composed the hymn "Take Me As I Am." We can come to God as we are. Be yourself and come as you are. Seek his grace and love. God will begin his work in you.

GOD SEES ME

> [6]"Your slave is in your hands," Abram said. "Do with her whatever you think best." Then Sarai mistreated Hagar; so she fled from her.
> [7] The angel of the Lord found Hagar near a spring in the desert; it was the spring that is beside the road to Shur. [8] And he said, "Hagar, slave of Sarai, where have you come from, and where are you going?"
> "I'm running away from my mistress Sarai," she answered.
> [9] Then the angel of the Lord told her, "Go back to your mistress and submit to her." [10] The angel added, "I will increase your descendants so much that they will be too numerous to count."
> [11] The angel of the Lord also said to her:
> "You are now pregnant
>   and you will give birth to a son.
> You shall name him Ishmael,
>   for the Lord has heard of your misery.
> [12] He will be a wild donkey of a man;
>   his hand will be against everyone
>   and everyone's hand against him,
> and he will live in hostility
>   towardall his brothers."
> [13] She gave this name to the Lord who spoke to her: "You are the God who sees me," for she said, "I have now seen the One who sees me." [14] That is why the well was called Beer Lahai Roi; it is still there, between Kadesh and Bered. (Gen 16:6–14)

Let me share a story of an air force pilot named Mark Anderson. This story is from a book Americans have loved, *Chicken Soup for the Soul*. Mark's wife, Susan, had lost her sight during an eye surgery. Imagine how frustrating and distraught she must be, to suddenly lose her vision. She had lost the ability to read books, get around the house, or go outside. Nothing would be as easy as before. Interestingly, Susan expressed a desire to continue to work when she completed rehabilitation. She wanted to work even though she couldn't see anymore. So Mark started to drive her to and from work. But after some weeks passed, he declared something to her rather coldly. He said that he couldn't help with the ride starting the very next day, so she would have to handle it on her own. This was disheartening to her. She probably felt anguish if she took this as his abandoning her when she was in need. But he was very firm.

Starting the next day, Susan faced the situation and somehow managed to get to and from work. She fell and ran into things. It was difficult but getting better with time. One day a bus driver said to her, "You have a good husband." She was shocked to hear it, so she asked what he meant. "You didn't know? Your husband always got on the bus with you, whenever you boarded." The truth of the matter was that her husband had been watching her. He thoughtfully helped her become independent.

We feel left alone when the going gets tough. But we would be reassured to know that someone's got our backs. We have such a helper. He always watches us, helps and saves us when we are in danger. It's no one other than our loving God. Sometimes people may play a similar role, like Mike Anderson did for his wife. But people have limits, as they might be distracted or fall asleep. Their help itself is inherently limited as well. God is different. The one who watches Israel neither gets sleepy nor falls asleep. Unlike people, God never gets distracted. We should get help from this God who never becomes negligent and provides perfect help to us. With God, we can run the race of life upright without falling down.

The Blessing of El Roi

Abram's wife, Sarai, couldn't get pregnant, so she had her servant, Hagar, bear a child through Abram. In fact, Sarai knew about God's promise. God had promised that Abram and Sarai would have offspring. But ten years passed in waiting. Even with big faith, this long of a wait would make one anxious. As there was no sign of a child as the body was aging, Sarai thought of a solution. It was to send Hagar to Abram to have a son. However, this was a deeply unfaithful move that brought about a disastrous consequence later. She failed to wait until God's appointed time and replaced his way with her own method.

We may feel that God's time seems too delayed to satisfy our thoughts and longing. The right faith would guide us to wait until God's time. If we try to take over control and rush to resolve a situation, it could lead to more problems and errors. It's also wrong that we get ahead of God's promise and interpret the situation as it pleases us. God had said that the offspring would come from Sarai's body. We must trust in God all the way. Perhaps Sarai doubted God's ability to carry out his promise. Because she doubted God, she decided to devise a solution on her own.

What was the outcome of Sarai's human choice? First, a seed of misfortune got impregnated. Hagar's son is Ishmael. Today he's regarded as the ancestor of the Muslims. The root of today's political and religious struggles goes all the way back to Hagar's pregnancy. Second, a feud began in Abram's family. The climate of family changed, as the previously obedient Hagar became proud with pregnancy. Sarai got annoyed and scolded Abram. Abram couldn't stand it and just transferred responsibility to Sarai, telling her to deal with Hagar however she wanted. From then on, Sarai began to abuse Hagar. We can conjecture that she probably abused Hagar both physically and emotionally. Hagar couldn't stand it anymore, and she ran away into the wilderness, pregnant with a baby.

All this unfortunate drama started with Sarai's unfaithful choice. Our lesson is to begin on the right note, in order to see through a beautiful ending. A faulty start makes it almost impossible to correct the course later on. In addition, a tradition of unfaith usually breeds a continuing bad cycle. In this case, it progressed from unfaithful pregnancy to family feud, to abuse, then to escape into the wilderness.

We can notice an important fact here. God was observing all this in the meantime. He saw Sarai drive out Hagar ruthlessly, as well as Hagar being driven out of home. God not only blessed and helped Abram home but also the lowly Hagar who ran away. God doesn't have favorites. He doesn't limit the blessings only to Abram or Israelites. His grace extends to a gentile female servant, a powerless and abused woman as well. Hagar then meets God's messenger in the desert. Here the messenger is God himself. Notice that God appeared before an unworthy servant of Egypt, not a chosen Israelite. He also helped her with direction of life and strengthened her.

Hagar calls God "El Roi," meaning "the God who sees me" in Hebrew. Other names of God in the bible include El Shaddai, Jehovah Shalom, and Jehovah-jireh. God watched her in crisis and helped her revive. Apply this to our lives. We sometimes have to endure a lonely, painful, and difficult time. Our "El Roi" always watches us. He will surely rescue and bless us.

God Prepares the Best

The characteristic of the blessing from El Roi is that it is the best. When we are lost, he shows us the best way. God's messenger asked Hagar who had left Sarai's home. "Sarai's servant girl, Hagar. Where are you from? And where are you headed?" This is the very question God asks us, too. Perhaps everyone wants to know the answer to this question. Where are we from and where are we going? God asked this while he knew us so well. Hagar responded, "I'm running from my master, Sarai."

By coincidence, the meaning of the name Hagar is also "fugitive (runaway)." The runaway, Hagar, pleads to God, "I wanted to stay but couldn't stand the master's abuse anymore." Hagar escaped problems as they came in her life. When misfortune knocked on her door, she even hid from it. Would problems go away if we kept giving up and running away from them? They wouldn't. God knew this very well and called Hagar. He challenges her to face it with faith. "Return to your master and obey." Here the "master" would be Sarai as well as the problem itself. In other words, God was telling Hagar to return to the very problem. And he commands her obedience to Sarai. The Message version of the Bible translates this passage as follows: "Put up with her abuse" (Gen 16:9). This is God's prescription. He told Hagar to stop escaping, to return to face the problem, then to endure it. Also, he promised to help her do this.

This is his way. From a human standpoint, it would make no sense. Yet God's way is ultimately right. Although it may seem reasonable and correct, a human way is crooked. Only God's way is correct. Only he knows our lives through and through. Thus, God's prescription is always the best.

David made the following confession about the all-knowing God. "You have searched me, Lord, and you know me" (Ps 139:1). In this verse, the word "search" also matches the characteristic of El Roi ("the one who sees"). God always searches us closely and knows us very well. David continues. "You know when I sit and when I rise; you perceive my thoughts from afar. You discern my going out and my lying down; you are familiar with all my ways. Before a word is on my tongue you, Lord, know it completely. You hem me in behind and before, and you lay your hand upon me" (Ps 139:2–5). Night and day he listens to us, even the whispers we say alone. Because he knows us inside out, he can protect us. Because he knows the front and back, the past and the future of our lives, his direction and guidance are always right. Just follow his direction even when it doesn't please or convince us. Go when he says to go. Stop when he says to stop. He is a responsible God who will always reward our obedience.

Here's a story of Bruce H. Wilkinson from pastor Chuck Swindoll's sermon. He was a conservative Baptist pastor who had graduated from a theological school in Dallas, Texas, and studied under a renowned professor, Howard G. Hendricks. His ministry of twenty-five years was to teach the Bible and develop and provide study materials that aid discipleship training (WTB: Walk Through the Bible). WTB became established all over the world and carried out a meaningful ministry to the thirsty. But after about twenty-five years passed, it began having some issues. A rumor about the leader of the ministry, Bruce Wilkinson, spread out of control, and he was on a brink of resignation. At that moment, God spoke to Wilkinson to go to Africa. It seemed out of the blue. Wouldn't it make more sense to stay in the US and sort out the problems? What would going to Africa have to do with this? He didn't understand, but he couldn't shake off God's strong conviction in his heart. He went to Africa.

When he arrived in Africa, he saw such misery of people stricken with AIDS. Thirteen million children had died of AIDS. The daily average death toll was at eight thousand. There was no solution in sight. No one could do anything. Bruce Wilkinson cried out to the Lord, "God, help us. We need money. Please provide money so that we can serve these people." He wrote a book, *The Prayer of Jabez*, which was published in 2000 and then became a worldwide bestseller. It was written out of his prayer and inspiration received from God. This small book stirred such high interests beyond imagination. He was able to found the Dream for Africa mission organization from the book sales and moved to Johannesburg to serve the African children.

People think it's all over when they see a dead end. This is not true. When a road ends, it's not over, because God opens a new road that he's prepared from there. When our plans fail, God's great plan can begin. Thus, we should obey him when he speaks to us. Go when he says to go. Stop when he says to stop. Just trust that God's way is the best, and he'll take responsibility for us. El Roi guides us on the best path forward.

He Prepares a Spring of Living Water

Another blessing from El Roi is that he provides a spring of living water for us. He not only provided the right direction to Hagar but also a spring so she wouldn't fall out of thirst. For someone who passes through the wilderness, the most urgent need wouldn't be materials like gold and silver, fame, or glory. He or she needs bread and food. But the most important need is actually water. Water is life in the desert. So God prepared a spring for Hagar. She experienced saving grace by this provision and named the spring "Beer-lahai-roi" (which means "well of the living one who sees me" in the original Hebrew text). The first part of the word means "spring," and the second part, lahai, means "life." "Roi" means "seeing," as in El Roi. So together, the spring's name means "the spring belonging to the living and watchful God."

In the wilderness of our lives, not just any spring would relieve us of thirst. Only the living God's spring would. We all need a Beer-lahai-roi. We will be truly revived. Take an example of many kinds of beverages. There are good beverages and unhealthy beverages. But in the end, any beverage of this world would make us thirsty again. No alternative can relieve us of our spiritual thirst but the Beer-lahai-roi.

Jesus met a Samarian woman at Sychar. Why did she come to the well in the middle of the day? She came to get some water at the well of Jacob. The well of Jacob is manmade. No matter whose name it takes after and how much we drink out of it, a manmade well would surely make us thirsty again. Take notice that the woman had a deep-seated thirst. She avoided people and came at noon. Jesus said to her, "Everyone who drinks this water will be thirsty again, but whoever drinks the water I give him will never thirst. Indeed, the water I give him will become in him a spring of water welling up to eternal life" (John 4:13–14). The water from Jesus is life-giving water. We should drink it to be alive. No matter how exhausted and dehydrated, we can recover after drinking his living water.

The same goes for church. The secret to church staying true and authentic in faith is this living water. The river of living water has to flow in church. It's not the same thing as having a good organizational structure or offering good programs for the congregation. Having a respectable building with many members in tens of thousands would not be sufficient to truly fulfill God's work. What church needs is his living water. And its essence is the gospel. True restorations and recoveries happen in the flowing presence of this living water of gospel.

The living water is also his power. Jesus said, "Whoever believes in me, as the Scripture has said, streams of living water will flow from within him" (John 7:38). Here the stream of living water refers to the Holy Spirit that we will receive. Do not run into the world when you face frustrating and difficult situations in life. I urge you to drink the living water instead. A tired soul will then be revived and start running again for God's calling. El Roi will show the best way and also provide the living water of eternity to the thirsty.

God Leads our Future

The last blessing from El Roi is to guide us with a direction into our future. We cannot know the future. No one knows what will happen. Only God determines our fate. There are people that believe in themselves. They believe they excavate life's path forward. But this is only a delusion when our own efforts don't fully control life. We cannot determine the future on our own. No amount of planning will govern the future events. All of this belongs to God. Only God's will can decide.

So was Ishmael's fate. The angel of the Lord said that he would become like a wild donkey of a man. A wild donkey refers to an undomesticated animal that runs about on its own in the wild. When one's life runs about like a wild donkey, he strikes himself, and everyone else also strikes him. In other words, it becomes a life of struggles and conflicts. "He will live in hostility toward all his brothers" (Gen 16:12). Ishmael's descendants are regarded as the Arab people living in the Middle East today. Take notice that Ishmael's future didn't sound so bright. It even looked bleak. In all of this, God was in control. Even Ishmael's descendants can be restored by God's grace. Actually we were just like them in the past. We once were gentiles outside of God's providence. Apostle Paul said, "Remember that at that time you were separate from Christ, excluded from citizenship in Israel and foreigners to the covenants of the promise, without hope and without God in the world" (Eph 2:12). Our identity changed completely when we met and accepted God. We were now God's children.

Do not try to be pioneers of your lives. Don't claim that "my life is my own." Instead, give your life to God. Through Jesus Christ, enter the gates of God's kingdom. Then God will certainly shine brightly on your path into the future.

Wayne Oates taught Christian ministry at a Southern Baptist Seminary in the United States. He told the following story. Many children became orphans after the World War II. War is especially cruel to the newborns and young children. Some orphans would not sleep at night and keep on weeping in sadness. They tried to comfort them back to sleep, or to discipline them to stop crying. But it didn't work. One observer proposed the following solution. "When children keep on weeping at night, offer them a piece of bread. They will stop crying." When they tried this, it actually worked. Let's think about why children couldn't go to sleep. They needed assurance about tomorrow. Parents can give that assurance. They don't need to worry about the next morning or survival. But the orphans don't have their parents, so they are anxious about tomorrow. A piece of bread provided hope to them and reassured them to sleep.

God promised that he wouldn't abandon us. God watches everyone, even the one who may feel all alone and miserable. Our God will never leave anyone empty-handed. He will pour love and grace. He will be our shepherd that guides us into the future. I sincerely wish that everyone meets this God. He knows our names, thoughts, tears, and pains, as he continuously watches over us and helps us when we are in need. Cry out to the Lord instead of running away. Problems and crises will dissipate with our strong faith in God. In the middle of the wilderness, a spring will break and we will dream a new future.

AN AWAKENING SOUND IN THE NIGHT OF LIFE

[1] The boy Samuel ministered before the Lord under Eli. In those days the word of the Lord was rare; there were not many visions.
[2] One night Eli, whose eyes were becoming so weak that he could barely see, was lying down in his usual place. [3] The lamp of God had not yet gone out, and Samuel was lying down in the house of the Lord, where the ark of God was. [4] Then the Lord called Samuel. Samuel answered, "Here I am." [5] And he ran to Eli and said, "Here I am; you called me."
But Eli said, "I did not call; go back and lie down." So he went and lay down.
[6] Again the Lord called, "Samuel!" And Samuel got up and went to Eli and said, "Here I am; you called me."
"My son," Eli said, "I did not call; go back and lie down."
[7] Now Samuel did not yet know the Lord: The word of the Lord had not yet been revealed to him.
[8] A third time the Lord called, "Samuel!" And Samuel got up and went to Eli and said, "Here I am; you called me."
Then Eli realized that the Lord was calling the boy. [9] So Eli told Samuel, "Go and lie down, and if he calls you, say, 'Speak, Lord,

for your servant is listening.'" So Samuel went and lay down in his place.
¹⁰ The Lord came and stood there, calling as at the other times, "Samuel! Samuel!"
Then Samuel said, "Speak, for your servant is listening."
(1 Sam 3:1–10)

Let me share an American folktale, "The Country Mouse and the City Cat." A mouse moved to a city because it was hard to make a living in the countryside. He expected to see some leftovers in the city.

On the first night that he arrived, an unexpected situation unfolded. He ran into a city cat in the middle of the night. The cat was also looking for food and jumped on the mouse as soon as he saw it. The mouse ran as fast as he could and managed to hide in a small hole behind a trash can. He silently waited for the cat to go away. A few moments later, a dog's bark was heard nearby. The mouse thought to himself, "Aha! The cat has left." He knew that a dog and a cat don't get along. Natural enemies cannot be in the same place, right? So the mouse felt relieved and got out of the hole. But to his surprise, the cat was still there, waiting. The mouse was so curious even at that moment of danger, that he asked if it was certainly a dog's bark then how could the cat still be there? The cat responded with a grin. "You got to be at least bilingual if you want to survive in this tough city."

This tough reality to the cat is not new to us, either. Using the analogy of time, life comes with a nighttime as dark as pitch black. We have to face such events, tragedies, or challenges that completely baffle and frustrate us. Against our wishes, this nighttime still comes inevitably.

The Voice of God in the Middle of Night

The chosen people of God, Israel, too faced a spiritually dark period. This was when the prophet Samuel was still a young boy. "The boy Samuel ministered before the Lord under Eli. In those days the word of the Lord was rare; there were not many visions" (1 Sam 3:1).

There are some typical symptoms of a spiritually dark period. Rarity of the word of the Lord is one of them. It's not that the word is not available. In the last times, the word may be available, yet it's mostly inauthentic. The prophet Amos said that the famine would come to Israel not because of a lack of food or water but because of their inability to listen to the words. Consider today's situation. We are surrounded by a more abundant presence of preaching and the word than before. We have access through TV, books, SNS, and other media. In the midst of the flood, there's no water that we can actually drink. Similarly, we can rarely find the true and authentic words in the last times.

Additionally, we can't find an "ideal" in a spiritually dark period. An ideal can also be expressed as a vision. It means there is no dream of the future. Only a completely dark reality of the present exists. We see the young adults having no flag to wave in an utter loss of direction, and this confirms the spiritually dark state of the present times.

Even the leaders lack good judgment and seem lost in this dark period. Eli, the priest of Israel, couldn't see well. It wasn't just due to his old age. His poor vision indicated deteriorating judgment as well. This was the dire reality Israel was facing. Nonetheless Israel had one hope. Look at verse 3 of 1 Sam 3: "The lamp of God had not yet gone out." Although everything else seemed pitch dark, God's lamp was still burning.

This reveals two contrasting meanings to us. First, the dawn has not come yet. It was expected that the lamp the priest lit the night before in the sanctuary would last through the next morning. In other words, it's still night. Before the dawn comes, it's still dark. Second, there is still hope. The lamp of God was still burning when all others had gone out. So as long as we come to the sanctuary before God, we can receive a new light.

Life is not over when all our ways are exhausted. Life is not over when our businesses close and various hardships and crises hit us. Life is not over yet when we get that diagnosis one day. In the sanctuary, the lamp of God is still burning. We only need courage to come forward to the sanctuary in our dark reality. Then we will hear his voice.

"Then the Lord called Samuel" (1 Sam 3: 4). On a personal level, God was calling Samuel to be a prophet in this passage. Simultaneously, God was also calling the Israelites to wake them up out of the darkness. God was calling bright morning to come to their history. Samuel's arrival announced a new beginning, the Kingdom Era. The prior period of the Judges was a time of confusion and disorder. People acted as they pleased. But now God's calling Samuel meant the end of the prior era, and the new beginning of the Kingdom Era.

We all need to hear this voice. We need to hear the voice coming from God, not from the world. We can conquer the darkness, when we follow his voice and re-illuminate our lives. Our lives will never be filled if we follow the voice of the world. Which voice are you betting your life on?

Sometimes, people's opinions and expertise can be of value. There are times when the opinions or advice of politicians or economists can be helpful. But these cannot be a solution to our dark times in life. Only God's voice can guide us through the dark night into the bright morning of blessings.

We need God's voice. The heavenly voice that resonates through the sanctuary alone will save us. Then what do we need to hear this voice?

Be in the Right Place

We have to be in the right place if we want to hear God's voice. Unless our spiritual state is in the right position, we will never hear it. Samuel heard God's voice in "his sanctuary," or the tabernacle to be more exact, as it was before a sanctuary was built. We have to be inside the tabernacle if we want to hear God. It's not possible if we are blended in the world, a place of pleasure and sin. When our hearts are right with God, in a clear position, we can then hear God. He speaks of our right place in the following way: "I am the vine; you are the branches. If you remain in me and I in you, you will bear much fruit; apart from me you can do nothing" (John 15:5).

Our lives will be aligned correctly when we abide in him. Then we will bear fruits and have a relationship with him. Many people wish for an abundant and thriving life, yet they don't attain it because they are not in the right place, despite futile efforts.

Joseph was sold as slave to Egypt when he was seventeen. But he still became a great ruler and influential of Egypt in his time. The secret to his success was not his good looks or luck. Joseph was like a tree planted by water. The branches grew out so strong that they went over the wall. His secret to success was that he was in the right place with God.

The Palestine region is barren. Even good seeds cannot grow well if water is not sufficient. Special desert trees such as tumble weeds can barely survive. On the other hand, if a good tree is planted by water, it will grow strong with green leaves and many fruits. Joseph didn't thrive because he was superior. It was because he was abiding in him. In the right place with God, our lives can thrive anywhere with such vitality.

Our place to be should be in Jesus Christ. No matter how much we possess in this world, a life outside of Jesus will never be a full, thriving one because one cannot meet or hear God. Then our important question to ourselves is, "Am I abiding in Jesus Christ?"

Let me share a professor's testimony that I heard some years ago. She lived in Korea and graduated from a top-tier university. She was from a good family and was a bright student, always doing well in school. She married a well-to-do businessman and continued to live a very comfortable life. She confessed that she had always been a churchgoer but never a truly reborn Christian. She thought that not going to church wouldn't be so bad, either. She was never desperate, as she always had good things in life. So church was more of a hobby or pastime.

Then one day her only daughter began to get ill. It only got worse, while many visits to different hospitals couldn't even uncover its diagnosis. She even brought the child to Japan for better treatment but to no avail. There was no way out, as the child was near death. Then she realized an important truth about life: that life cannot be controlled as one wishes. She thought money could buy and solve things previously. Her PhD was useless, too. She kneeled down before God and started repenting. She repented her arrogance that she could live without him.

Her prayer of repentance continued on for months, then a deaconess visited her. She had heard of this heartbreaking situation and came to pray for her family. She simply came to offer consolation and comfort, as she didn't have special gifts such as healing. So she prayed with her hand on the child's head then went back. Amazingly the child began to get better after the prayer. She recovered from the terminal illness. After this incident, the professor truly changed and became a follower of Jesus.

We need intellect and money. But a true life only comes from Jesus. Unless we abide in Jesus Christ, no amount of efforts and possessions can bring us to the place of true life. To hear God's voice, we have to find the right place, which is in Jesus Christ. Only there we can begin a new life and start a relationship with God.

Have a Spiritual Focus

We have to have a spiritual focus to hear God's voice. Our hearts should be centered on God. In fact, Samuel hadn't realized that it was God calling him. He didn't catch on from get-go. God called Samuel three times, and Samuel ran over to Eli, thinking he was calling. It's not easy to decipher a voice coming from God. It was not easy even for a person residing inside a sanctuary like Samuel. Then how hard would it be for us, living busy lives immersed in this world? It's never easy to decipher God's voice. It requires our full focus on him.

In modern times, so many things distract us. It's never easy to focus on something. We may become disheartened after unexpected, devastating life events. Sometimes we may get deep emotional wounds from simple, careless words from someone. It's quite common that we want to get some comfort from people but end up getting hurt instead. One thoughtless or hurtful comment can stab us deeply. Although unintentional, a careless word can disperse one's heart. Let us not be distracted by the surroundings and fully focus on God to hear him.

Elijah was a great prophet, but he also was spiritually exhausted one time. In the peak times of idolatry during the King Ahab's reign, Elijah confronted the followers of Baal and revealed God's glory. He was truly a brave and honorable prophet. However, briefly after his victory at Mount of Carmel, he became discouraged. He heard that Jezebel threatened his life. He became afraid and ran into the wilderness. He sat under a broom tree and asked that he might die. This meant that a Lord's servant declared a spiritual suicide. He asked that his life be taken away, as he had done enough. This may be the most incomprehensible passage in 1 Kgs 17–19.

Consider again who Elijah was. He was a hero who won against 850 followers of Baal at Mount of Carmel in such a dark era. When rain had stopped for three years and six months, he prayed seven times at the top of Mount Carmel, and his faith brought rain. How could it be that the same Elijah became so weak by Queen Jezebel's threat that he prayed for his own death? The short answer is his spiritual exhaustion. This could happen to anyone who becomes occupied with ministries and loses focus on God. You may run very hard but end up falling out of complete exhaustion.

Elijah was like this and God restored him. First, he fed him. God didn't send him away somewhere. He let him gather strength by eating. After that, God sent him to Mount Horeb, where God was present. When he stood on Mount Horeb, the Lord passed by. A great and strong wind tore the mountains and broke in pieces the rocks before the Lord, but the Lord was not in the wind (1 Kings 19). And after the wind an earthquake, but the Lord was not in the earthquake. And after the earthquake a fire, but the Lord was not in the fire. And after the fire the sound of a low whisper (1 Kings 19). We may expect God's presence in some extraordinary events, but this is only a prejudice and wrongful assumption. God speaks in a whisper.

God spoke regarding a job that Elijah had to do. The Lord said to him, "Go, return on your way to the wilderness of Damascus. And when you arrive, you shall anoint Hazael to be king over Syria. And Jehu the son of Nimshi you shall anoint to be king over Israel, and Elisha the son of Shaphat of Abel-meholah you shall anoint to be prophet in your place." God also comforted Elijah, saying, "I will leave seven thousand in Israel, all the knees that have not bowed to Baal, and every mouth that has not kissed him" (1 Kgs 19). Elijah was able to recover after he heard God and completed his ministry. In our lives, too, God speaks to us in a whisper. To those who focus and yearn for God's voice, he lets them hear it.

Pastor Lawrence Khong (Lead Pastor of Faith Community Baptist Church in Singapore) once shared some difficult experiences from his early ministry days. His church had started with around three hundred regular members, and the attendance kept declining. For some reason, members were leaving the church week after week. Falling attendance is really a serious concern to the pastor. Generally in this kind of situation, the pastor is blamed. He had to suffer not only the pain of church members leaving but also the criticisms coming from the congregation.

One day he was reading Mark 1:9–11 in the Bible. Jesus just had been baptized by John in the Jordan river. "Just as Jesus was coming up out of the water, he saw heaven being torn open and the Spirit descending on him like a dove. And a voice came from heaven: 'You are my Son, whom I love; with you I am well pleased'" (Mark 1:10–11). In that moment of reading this verse, he felt as if God was right in front of him and speaking this to him. "Are church members leaving? It's alright. My son, I love you. I'm pleased with you. Do people blame and criticize you? Do not worry. My son, I love you. I'm pleased with you."

No matter how damaged your heart and reputation are by people, it is enough when God assures you to not worry. It is enough if he loves you and he is pleased with you. This voice of God strengthened him to get back up. We all need this voice. We have to listen to the encouraging voice of God, not the harsh voice of critics. We cannot bet our lives on what other people think of us. God deems us precious. With his voice, our soul can get back up. We can keep dreaming God's dream and continue to bear our ministries with joy. We need to focus our hearts to God, so we can hear him.

Obeying

We have to obey in order to hear God's voice. He allows us to hear when we obey. Would it be unnecessary to speak to the disobeying when it's obvious that it wouldn't be followed? God speaks to the willfully obedient.

Young Samuel finally realized that it was God calling. "Speak, Lord, for your servant is listening." He was ready to listen. To those who are willing to listen to God and obey, God will speak and let his works begin.

Countless people are mentioned in the Old Testament. God used Abraham for a simple reason. Abraham unconditionally obeyed God. He obeyed openly. He didn't measure, calculate, or weigh options. He just followed. When told to go, stand, sleep, or eat, then he would go, stand, sleep, or eat as told. Abraham's obedience pleased God. So he endowed him with grace and power of his words.

Why did God use the prophet Isaiah? When God asked who would go on behalf of them, Isaiah responded, "Lord, I'm here. Send me." This pleased God, and he showed his wondrous works to him.

Even in our times, God is looking for people who will follow him with obedience. He looks for our obedience, not our achievements or money. Human ability is always limited. We do not work with our limited ability. When we obey, God will enable us to complete the work. It is my sincere wish that church members increase in number with those who are willing to follow and obey.

Let me share a story I heard from a professor who was at a KOSTA conference some years ago. A wealthy man in Texas invited a whole village to his house. In his swimming pool, hundreds of piranha fish were released. They are known to be carnivorous fish. He proposed to the crowd. Whoever jumps into the pool and makes it across to the other end, will receive half of his wealth. A young man immediately jumped into the water. Piranha instantly gathered around him and ate his flesh. Although his body was bitten and became bloody, he still made it across successfully.

Then the wealthy man asked him, "Do you want half of my wealth or my daughter?" He replied, gasping. "I don't want your money or daughter. I want to find the one who pushed me into the water." The young man didn't jump into the water at his own will.

In churches, too, there are people jumping into works because someone pushed them. But God is pleased with voluntary people's dedication. These people can obey him. If we love him, we need to express it. By doing our best in obedience to God's commands, we can build up the churches and his kingdom.

Pastor Jack Graham (Lead Pastor of Prestonwood Baptist Church in Texas) has a sermon broadcast. He once shared his own testimony from childhood. He frequently passed by a big house, and in it there was a scary dog. It was aggressive towards strangers. He used to run away from it out of fear. Walking by that house was a fearful experience. He even took a long detour to avoid it. One day he told his dad about this. His dad advised, "Jack, next time the dog barks at you, do not run. When it intimidates you, look straight into its eyes. Then it'll never be able to hurt you."

He felt afraid but gave it a shot the way his dad told him. He did look straight into the barking dog's eyes. How would the dog have reacted? It was even more agitated and furious at this daring rebellion of the boy. A moment later, the dog somehow collapsed to the ground. It turned out that it was tied with a thick chain. His dad knew this and encouraged him to be not afraid, with a winning strategy.

Similarly, we may be facing a daunting situation and the enemies in the world may be attacking us furiously. We are inclined to be afraid and run. But remember that God already chained all our enemies. We need not be afraid. All we need to do is simply listen and follow him. In faith, we must look onto him and proceed toward his will. We will surely break through the dark and live a victorious life when we focus to listen and follow him.

The night of our lives may not be over. We may have many unresolved problems. They could be related to family, finances, or uncertain futures to list a few. However, we must not give up out of worry or fear. The lamp of God is still burning. When we trust him and come before his sanctuary, we will find his light. The victory will be ours at his throne of glory. We should bet our lives on his voice. Never give up, and keep running towards his glory.

2

In the Middle of Night, the Lamp of God Has Not Gone Out

[12] So I will always remind you of these things, even though you know them and are firmly established in the truth you now have. [13] I think it is right to refresh your memory as long as I live in the tent of this body, [14] because I know that I will soon put it aside, as our Lord Jesus Christ has made clear to me. [15] And I will make every effort to see that after my departure you will always be able to remember these things.

[16] For we did not follow cleverly devised stories when we told you about the coming of our Lord Jesus Christ in power, but we were eyewitnesses of his majesty. [17] He received honor and glory from God the Father when the voice came to him from the Majestic Glory, saying, "This is my Son, whom I love; with him I am well pleased."[a] [18] We ourselves heard this voice that came from heaven when we were with him on the sacred mountain.

[19] We also have the prophetic message as something completely reliable, and you will do well to pay attention to it, as to a light shining in a dark place, until the day dawns and the morning star rises in your hearts. [20] Above all, you must understand that no prophecy of Scripture came about by the prophet's own interpretation of things. [21] For prophecy never had its origin in the human will, but prophets, though human, spoke from God as they were carried along by the Holy Spirit.

—2 PET 1:12–21

WHAT WILL WE BET OUR LIVES ON?

A farmer in America had been gambling at horse racing for more than a few decades. He wanted a big jackpot but only kept losing. One day the horse he bet on came in first. The prize money was a whopping two hundred million dollars. The government did some research on him before disbursing the big amount. They found that the winner was a very poor farmer. They worried that he might get a heart attack at the news of a huge winning beyond his reach.

So they thought of a clever alternative, which was to give the prize to the priest of his town (the farmer was a Catholic). The priest was conversing with the farmer. "I heard that you bet your money again on horse racing. If you ever won the first prize, what would you do with it?" The farmer responded unenthusiastically. "There's no way it's going to happen to me. I've gambled for more than a few decades, but never won." Then the priest said. "Hypothetically, if you won about two hundred million dollars in prize, what would you do?" The farmer pondered for a minute and said, "If I won such money, I would give half of it to you. . ." Before he could finish his sentence, the priest had a heart attack, not the farmer.

Everyone has something they value enough to bet their lives on. It could be money, academic achievements, or the luck of winning a big jackpot such as lotto or gambling. Do any of these guarantee lasting happiness? Never. These are just phenomena and trends of this world. They appear enticing, but in reality, they are dangerous. They often result in emptiness of life. It would be risky to bet our lives on uncertain and volatile things in the world. They may leave us any minute. Our lives will be much safer and fulfilled if we invest on one sure and safe being that is totally worthy of our lives from the present into the future.

Is there any supreme being in whom we can invest our entire lives with total confidence? It's Jesus Christ and his gospel. Everything we pursue belongs in him. The true way and the true life are in him. Our livelihood belongs in his cross. If you want your life to be worthy and beautiful, come to the root of all blessings, Jesus Christ, and invest all in him. Then we will bear valuable fruits, firmly rooted in his words.

Betting Our Lives on the Gospel

What do we need to commit ourselves fully to Jesus Christ and the gospel? A deciding moment for apostle Peter was when he met Jesus Christ and the truth of the gospel. Peter lived for the gospel all his life and wanted the witnessed to stand strong in the truth. He wrote to the members of church in a letter, "So I will always remind you of these things, even though you know them and are firmly established in the truth you now have" (2 Pet 1:12). By "them," Peter means from the prior verse, "receiving a rich welcome into the eternal kingdom of our Lord and Savior Jesus Christ" (2 Pet 1:11). In short, "them" means salvation. He wanted to keep reminding them of this knowledge of the gospel.

Why would he keep reminding of the salvation when the saved brothers and sisters of church were well aware of it? Foremost, it was to deter the attack from the false teachers. False teaching that bent or stole truth had penetrated into church. The book of 2 Peter was written to defend against those false teachings. For this reason, the truth of the gospel needed to be continually emphasized.

Another reason was that Christians were not living the gospel. It's not that they don't know what the truth is in their heads. They needed the reminders to help live it out in practice. Sermons are essentially the repeated reminders or instructions that help Christians live out faith, as William Barclay said.

The repetitions were necessary for the truth to be properly understood and internalized in people's lives. First, Peter decided to wake up Christians "while they were in the tent." A tent meant temporary housing. People in the ancient Israel didn't have permanent homes, as they lived a nomadic life. They moved around and set up temporary tents. These are like our physical bodies. Our bodies are the temporary houses for our souls.

Peter knew to diligently remind them of the truth of the gospel while he was alive physically. He didn't pay much attention to other matters. He poured all into Jesus Christ and his ministry. He wanted members of church to remember the truth any time after he died. He sincerely wished the solidifying of the knowledge of the gospel to outlive him.

Actually a book of gospel has survived Peter's passing. It's the book of Mark. While Mark wrote this book, Peter told him about the life and ministry of Jesus. Mark was not a direct disciple of Jesus. He did not see Jesus' works or hear his words firsthand. But Mark was still able to record in this book as he remembered what Peter told him. Some early fathers of

Christianity such as Irenaeus and Papias had called the book of Mark the book of Peter for this reason. Additionally, the book of Mark is the basis for all the other Gospel books. Most theologians agree that it was the earliest written Gospel book. The word "Gospel" was also used for the first time in the book of Mark. Gospel is a different genre from historic accounts, praises, or letters. The book of Mark started it.

Again Peter's top priority was to teach and remind Christians of the truth of gospel to last beyond his lifetime and generation. For this cause, he lived and died. His teachings still remain to this day in the book of Mark. Coming from a humble background, as he was a countryside fisherman in Galilee, he was used by God in such a worthy and honored way in the Christian history.

Let us not stop short by hearing the gospel and getting saved ourselves. We should go further and commit our lives wholly for Jesus Christ and his gospel. God has a purpose for our lives. He wants us to live for the everlasting gospel. The direction of our lives will be well aligned with God, and we will leave behind glorious fruits. The same goes for church. What makes church "church" would be the passion of the gospel. We should re-examine whether the gospel can be sidelined by other agendas, dishonoring the glory of God. How can we run the race in faith so we live without regrets? Let us look at some spiritual traits of Peter that we can model ourselves after.

Surrendering

We need faith to surrender our lives to God. Peter gained a new perspective on life and death. "Because I know that I will soon put it aside, as our Lord Jesus Christ has made clear to me" (2 Pet 1:14). Here "it" refers to the tent or his body. He was aware of his impending death. He expected he would be arrested and persecuted by the Romans. He said, "Jesus Christ made clear to me." So he believed that his physical life will end at a specified point in time by Jesus. Peter followed Jesus wholeheartedly. Had he lived with partial or compromised faith, he probably wouldn't have been able to recognize God's timing for his death.

Jesus had hinted at his death to Peter, prior to the crucifixion. "When you were younger you dressed yourself and went where you wanted; but when you are old you will stretch out your hands, and someone else will dress you and lead you where you do not want to go" (John 21:18). He prophesied about Peter's death. This verse may sound unpleasant at first, but it provides positive assurance. First, Peter wouldn't die at a young age. He would certainly die when old. They estimate that Peter probably heard this in his thirties. He later died in his sixties. So he wouldn't need to worry about death for about thirty years. No matter what hardships may come, he wouldn't die early. Accordingly, Peter lived until his time without worry about death.

In fact, Peter was in jail at the time apostle James was persecuted to death during the reign of King Herod Agrippa I. The persecution gained momentum as the Jews cheered on. Peter was shackled at the ankles between two soldiers in the jail and was awaiting his death by beheading the next morning. He was peacefully sleeping that night. Yes, the night before his persecution, he might have even snored off. He was so deeply asleep that an angel who came to rescue had to poke his sides. This is unbelievable. Who can possibly sleep so relaxed right before the beheading? Yet Peter did. Some might say it's just his personality, but I highly doubt that. More likely, he must have remembered God's prophesy that he would die at old age. He must have known that it was too early for him to die. He probably believed that God would somehow rescue him in time before the persecution. This is an example of surrendering in faith.

Environments do not matter. The level of complexity of the situation does not matter. Even if you are chained and scheduled to be beheaded the next morning, it still does not matter. The surrendering faith conquers the fear of death. Trusting God's words and coming before him in peace exemplify the surrendering faith. When we leave all in God's hands, nothing shakes us. In that firm trust in the responsible God, we don't get distressed in the face of despairing events.

Peter was not afraid of death as an event itself. "I will make every effort to see that after my departure you will always be able to remember these things" (2 Pet 1:15). This verse foretold a departure (by death) or farewell. In Greek, "exodus" was used. It means "opening a road" or "leaving a road." The book of Exodus also used the same word, as it captured the story of Israelites departing from Egypt and leaving behind their bondage. The exodus of Israelites meant moving from Egypt to the promised land.

Peter looked at death that way. He thought death transports us from this place to another. Many people believe death equals losing all. Peter had hope in the heaven. To him, death would take him from this troubled life to heaven, as exodus moved Israelites from bondage in Egypt into the promised land. Hence, death would be a part of God's promise. With this mindset, no one would be afraid of death.

If we believe that we belong to God whether alive or dead, nothing can make us afraid or worried. In today's world, people cannot stop worrying because they are occupied with this present life. They constantly worry about what to eat and wear, as they are only occupied with this physical life. But if we believe with Peter's mindset, we can rest assured that God will take responsibility and lead any situation in life. We can be victorious in the surrendering faith.

Experiential Spirituality

We need experiential spirituality to commit fully to a faith-centered life. We need to not only surrender all problems to the Lord but also experience him on a personal level. Hearing about him is not enough. Through experience, we can internalize faith.

"For we did not follow cleverly devised stories when we told you about the coming of our Lord Jesus Christ in power, but we were eyewitnesses of his majesty" (2 Pet 1:16). To reiterate, the coming of our Lord Jesus Christ in power is not a cleverly devised story. The heart of the gospel entails the power of Jesus Christ that was revealed in his miracles and ministries and the resurrection event. A "cleverly devised story" refers to a fake story or fable. The gospel of Jesus is not some fake story.

The word "myth" originated from a Greek word, "muthos." Greek people loved myths. The gods of the Greek were the main themes of myths. Myths are fiction without historic roots or evidence. On the other hand, the gospel of Jesus is not a myth. It's based in history. Jesus existed in history. He lived on this land. His crucifixion and resurrection are also real historic events because there were witnesses. Because the Lord promised to return, this will be a real historic event which will be fulfilled, not a fictional anticipation.

Peter introduced his own encounter with God to help verify the gospel to be a real, factual event in history. "He received honor and glory from God the Father when the voice came to him from the Majestic Glory, saying, 'This is my Son, whom I love; with him I am well pleased.' We ourselves heard this voice that came from heaven when we were with him on the sacred mountain" (2 Pet 1:17–18). He described his experience on the sacred mountain. Jesus Christ took three of his disciples—Peter, James, and

John—up on a mountain where Moses and Elijah appeared and Jesus was transfigured. His face and clothes became dazzlingly bright. This was a preview of the upcoming resurrection and its glory. Although very brief, Peter witnessed Jesus' transfiguration and heard his voice firsthand. This must have been a truly extraordinary and incomparable experience.

After having such a spiritual experience, you can have a firm conviction and pass on the gospel to others. Christian faith is not entirely theory or theology. It becomes your personal experience as well. We cannot be witnesses of gospel without our own encounter with God. How can we introduce something when we only know it at some abstract level? We ourselves have to meet God. Then we can witness him.

Faith in God is not entirely theoretical. It's not an abstract thought process. Rather, it involves our experiencing the living God. Accordingly, David said, "Taste and see that the Lord is good" (Ps 34:8). No transformation can occur before personally experiencing God. If we want to serve him, we need to experience him. His touches in our life experiences can help us share powerful testimonies when sharing the good news. We can cope with crises with composure. Thus, I encourage all of us to come before God daily and meet him personally. I encourage all of us to accumulate the wealth of spiritual secrets with God as we keep on hearing his voice and experiencing his touch. Then we can run on the right track to the life that pleases God.

Spirituality of the Gospel

To commit fully to the life of gospel, we also need the spirituality of the gospel. "We also have the prophetic message as something completely reliable, and you will do well to pay attention to it, as to a light shining in a dark place, until the day dawns and the morning star rises in your hearts" (2 Pet 1:19). By "something completely reliable," he meant a message that was even more assured than the experience of witnessing the transfiguration of Jesus at the Sacred Mountain. He meant the Bible. More specifically, he referred to the prophecy about the messiah in Scripture. We need personal experiences as well as the immutable and timeless source of authority.

Scripture is the lamp onto darkness. Without true light, this period is dark and confused. The Bible is the only and absolute light of truth in this lost age. In the middle of a dark night, we need to pay attention to this lamp until his return.

"Above all, you must understand that no prophecy of Scripture came about by the prophet's own interpretation of things. For prophecy never had its origin in the human will, but prophets, though human, spoke from God as they were carried along by the Holy Spirit" (2 Pet 1:20–21). No other verse captures the nature of prophesy in Scripture like this one. Scripture was recorded by men but originally came from God. The book of Matthew was written by Matthew and that of Luke by Luke. The epistles of Paul were written by Paul. The majority of psalms in the Old Testament were composed by David. Why do we call them the words of God when men wrote these?

It's because "all Scripture is God-breathed" (2 Tim 3:16) and men wrote, inspired by the Holy Spirit.

Thus we should not subjectively interpret Scripture. We should take extreme caution about each and every word in the Bible and follow the guidance of the Holy Spirit in order to properly understand it. Scripture shines light onto our lives in this dark and confused world. No one else can lead us to the absolute truth. Everything is relative. However, Jesus Christ alone can lead us to the absolute truth. Only his words are the true guide that shines light and leads us out of darkness.

Not a single thing is certain in our lives. The materials or fame we enjoy today could leave us any minute. The healthy bodies we rely on could get sick any minute. We may be confident today, but no one can know what the future holds. But we can be assured that Jesus and his gospel will stand firm and worthy of our entire lives. We won't be ashamed of Jesus and our lives dependent on him. We can live out his will and purpose in us, defeating any obstacles, if we let him be our Lord. He is the source of all power, resources, and blessings.

There is an eight-year-old girl named Hye-rin at my church. She was hospitalized due to leukemia and lost consciousness. While she was in a coma, her body weakened, and it got harder to breathe. The doctor already announced her impending death to her parents. He advised to remove the child's oxygen mask and send her off peacefully. It was time for the parents to get ready. Could you imagine how her parents must have felt? What can we possibly cling to in a situation like this? Can a doctor heal the child? Can pharmaceutical drugs aid her? We can only hold onto Jesus Christ. There is nothing else left, except for surrendering the situation to him and praying. The whole congregation of my church prayed together for a week, then Hye-rin woke up. She was transferred to a regular recovery room; her oxygen mask removed, she even blinked and shed tears. God worked a miracle.

We ourselves are unable to take control of our lives. Do not bet your lives on yourselves. Do not bet on power, wealth, or connections. They cannot take care of our lives all the way. No doctor, politician, or economist can bear responsibility of our lives. Only the resurrected Jesus can. We are only fragile like clayware, yet with living Jesus in us, we can get back up and run the race towards his glory.

THE CROSSROADS

[15] They have left the straight way and wandered off to follow the way of Balaam son of Bezer, who loved the wages of wickedness. [16] But he was rebuked for his wrongdoing by a donkey—an animal without speech—who spoke with a human voice and restrained the prophet's madness. [17] These people are springs without water and mists driven by a storm. Blackest darkness is reserved for them. [18] For they mouth empty, boastful words and, by appealing to the lustful desires of the flesh, they entice people who are just escaping from those who live in error. (2 Pet 2:15–18)

The Program is a movie about Lance Armstrong, a famous American cyclist. Armstrong is one of the most accomplished and decorated athletes in the American sports history. When he was twenty-five years old in 1996, he was diagnosed with testicular cancer, a rare form of cancer. It was a death sentence as it was already in the late stage when found. The cancerous cells had spread from lungs to abdomen, then to his brain with only a low 20 percent chance of survival. It seemed hopeless. But Armstrong didn't give up and started fighting it. Eventually he survived it against the odds. Only three years after, in 1999, Armstrong decided to participate in the Tour de France, an annual men's bicycle race.

The race lasts three weeks and entails three thousand kilometers of rough terrain. It is deservingly nicknamed "the Race in Hell." Armstrong made history in this race. He was the first non-European to win. After that initial win, he consecutively won six more times until 2005. Lance Armstrong became an unmatched sports hero, gained popularity, and became really rich. In short, he rose to the pinnacle of success. Then he fell straight down to the bottom and lost his reputation. It was discovered that he used drugs at every Tour de France that he participated in. In 2012, he was stripped of all seven of the champion titles, and his name got removed dishonorably from the world of sports. He used an illegal shortcut to get ahead of others.

We often use the analogy of a journey to describe our lives. Depending on which path we take, our fruits and benefits will vary. Most of all, our final destinations will be different. Thus, we have to choose the right path. However, these days people tend to take the fast route, not the right one. They believe they succeed when they get ahead of others and gain lots of money. They don't mind bending or breaking rules to be faster than others. Beware the hefty consequences of not running ethically. You may get to the top fast, but the sweet success will be short-lived and taken away dishonorably.

We should learn how to run our race the right way, not the fast way. This would be even more crucial for the followers of Jesus, to set the right example in this world. We should ask ourselves how we can choose the right path that pleases God in this broken and confused world.

What We Need to Make the Right Choice

Some people were rebuked by God in the Bible because they got sidetracked and chose the wrong path. False teachers were such an example. They followed the way of Balaam, son of Beor. This was deviating from the right path. Then what was the way of Balaam? Numbers 22–24 explains it. The Israelites camped at the plains of Moab after exiting Egypt and crossing the wilderness. Canaan was within reach if they only crossed the Jordan River. At that moment, King Balaak was devising a plan against the invasion of Israel. He knew that Israel had won battles against the gentiles with a mighty power. He was afraid of Israel, so he searched for ways to win his battle before the Israelites arrived. He thought of the prophet Balaam and asked him to curse them.

Pethor (where Balaam lived) was in the upper Euphrates River region, which was about four hundred miles from the Moab plains. Balaam was probably a sorcerer living in the gentile land. Then he met God personally. He came to know, commune with him, and understand his will. King of Moab sent gold, silver, and his officials to Balaam, as a gratuity for his astrology. In short, Balaam sent a payment in return for a favor, which was to curse the Israelites. Balaam declines this request. He knew that it was not God's will, and it should not be manipulated by some witchcraft or fortune-telling.

Then King Balaak sent even more treasures and officials. He even offered a high and prestigious position to Balaam as a reward. Balaam, then, asked for one day's time. Perhaps he was enticed by the good offer. That night he was going to ask God and give an answer the following day. We may ask whether it's really necessary to ask this question to God, as it involves cursing people using trickery. Of course, for some problems in life, we might have to pray long until we receive his direction. But for this particular problem that Balaam faced, it wouldn't really be necessary, as it involved cursing God's people using ungodly crafts. For example, would we need to pray long and hard about whether we should lie? Clearly, there is no need to pray long and hard about committing crimes such as extramarital affairs, murder, and theft, either. We should know to do what is right. Yet Balaam asked God. This implies that his heart was already leaning the wrong way. As a result, Balaam left behind negative influence that harmed Israel as well as himself.

He made a foolish mistake because he was tempted by money. This was the way of Balaam. An easy and fast shortcut to wealth and success, although not legitimate and ethical, is the way of Balaam. Following Balaam makes people lose their conscience, ignore God, and only focus on satisfying their own desires. In other words, the way of Balaam is the wrong, crooked way, which God is displeased with. Nonetheless, countless people choose this path to easily attain what they want. When all the others follow the way of Balaam, we should be different. If we are followers of Jesus, we should never choose the wrong way for short-term, immediate gains.

We must remember one important fact. Blessings are present on the right path, not the fast one. This is an unchanging rule. The right path may appear long-winding, but eventually it will be the faster one because God accompanies us. For individuals and churches alike, we should take the right road for the fruits of blessings. How can Christians choose the right path in this broken and confused world? Let us look at some key principles to help us make the right choice.

The Right Desire

The desire of our hearts should be right in order to choose the right way. What does it mean to have the right desire? The person or object that your desire points to should be right. The right desire leads to the right path. The main driver of Balaam's wrong choice was "loving the payment for unrighteousness." Here the "payment for unrighteousness" means unfair reward or unlawful gain. Balaam "loved" it. In Greek, "love" is agapao, from which the well-known noun form, agape, came. It means full devotion. It's not liking or being infatuated to some moderate degree. It implies losing your whole heart. God loves us this whole-hearted way. Thus we should love God in an agape style. However, Balaam replaced God with material gain in his agape. This teaches us the importance of keeping God at the center of our hearts. We may have some religious titles or act like perfect Christians in front of others, yet if the center of our hearts is occupied by something else, then we cannot hear God. Even if we hear it, we will disobey.

Human choices and behavior all originate from the heart. The passion inside, and what is taking over the heart, will determine one's behavior. Thus, we should have the right desire at heart. If our hearts are filled with financial motivations, we have to follow in the direction of financial gains. If they are filled with pleasure, we have to pursue the pleasures of the body. But if they are filled with God, our behavior will also follow our agape love for God. Our desire at heart should be right.

A shooting incident happened at the Immanuel Church in Charleston, South Carolina, on June 17, 2015. This church was founded by a black pastor, a former slave, in 1816. It was also the oldest black church in the southern United States. On that day, a white young man entered the church and shot nine people. These included Pastor Clementa Pinkney and members of the church who were gathered for Bible study. The criminal kept shooting many rounds at the victims who had already been shot and dead. Why did this happen? First, it did not happen by mistake or coincidence. It was a hate crime. It was triggered by racism and prejudice that the white man's mind was occupied with for a long time. His mind and heart were filled with racial bias and hate.

On the contrary, the families of the victims behaved very differently. It was evident that they kept God in their hearts instead of hate and resentment. On the first day at the court, both the criminal and the victims' families showed. They could see his face clearly. We can only imagine how they felt, seeing the heartless murderer of their loved ones.

A normal reaction would have been showing rage, screaming at him, or grabbing him by the neck. However, they did not behave that way. All the surviving family members declared to forgive the shooter.

The mother of Tywanza Sanders, a shooting victim, shared this deeply touching confession. Tywanza Sanders had graduated from college last year and planned on opening a barber shop to support his family. He was a twenty-six-year-old young black man who regularly attended the church Bible study. Although he was poor, he had hope and a dream. Then all his hope got shattered by a racist's gun. His mother confessed, "We welcomed you Wednesday night in our Bible study with welcome arms. You have killed some of the most beautiful people that I know. Every fiber in my body hurts and I'll, I'll never be the same. Tywanza Sanders was my son. But Tywanza Sanders was my hero. Tywanza was my hero. . . . May God have mercy on you."[1]

It's not a confession just anyone can do. Perhaps it might be remotely possible after ten years pass for some. But how could she give such a confession within a matter of a few days? It's undoubtedly hard to forgive the murderer who took away your loved one's life. We can only explain this with God's presence in the center of her heart. It's truly the power of faith.

When God is at the center of our hearts, we can forgive the unforgivable and accept the unacceptable. Our mourning and grief can turn into gratitude and praise. If we want to walk properly as Christians, we should let God reign in our hearts. Our spirit should be filled with God's love and passion, so we can run our race on the right track.

The Right Perspective

The next thing we need is the right perspective. We need our eyes to see properly, as well as our hearts. As Balaam refused to go God's way, something appeared to block him. It was not a person but a donkey. "The Lord opened the donkey's mouth, and it said to Balaam" (Num 22) to oppose the prophet's reckless ways.

So Balaam became the first prophet rebuked by a donkey. The donkey said that Balaam's behavior was "reckless." What a disgrace this is for a prophet! Even though he knew it didn't agree with God's will, he got up in the morning and saddled his donkey to pursue material gain. At that time, the angel of the Lord stood in the road with a drawn sword in his hand. He was there to oppose Balaam. While Balaam didn't see the angel, his donkey did. So it left the road and jumped into the field. Unaware of this situation, Balaam got angry and beat the donkey repeatedly. Not once or twice, he beat it three times. Then the donkey finally opened his mouth to rebuke him. It's truly outrageous and disgraceful.

1. Izadi, Elahe. "The Powerful Words of Forgiveness Delivered to Dylann Roof by Victims' Relatives." *Washington Post*, Jun 19, 2015.

Fittingly Skip Heitzig, a theologian, commented that Balaam was inducted into the Old Testament Hall of Shame. Compare this with the "Hall of Fame" that marks the excellence of individuals and their achievements. Balaam became a Hall of Shamer. His spiritual eyesight was terrible. He didn't catch what a donkey saw. When materials occupy our mind and heart, we don't see God, as if scales are covering our eyes.

Paul had the following experience when he was young. He became blind for three days after encountering the resurrected Jesus in person. Paul had persecuted Christians with his cause that he served God. His vision or perspective was covered by legalism of the Pharisees. God sent Ananias to lay hands on him and restore his sight. From this moment on, Paul began to see the road of gospel and ministry as a Christian.

Our eyes, too, can be covered with scales. For example, scales of greed can cover our sight, making our conscience invisible. If the scales of arrogance and selfishness cover our eyes, we cannot see humility. There are too many types of scales that block our sights to see good traits of humanity. To list just a few more, the scales of vanity, falsehood, or pretense exist. When we remove all the scales off our eyes, we can then see God and his spiritual realm. If you are yet unable to see his world, I encourage you to come before God. You need the touch of the Holy Spirit.

Ask the Holy Spirit to open your sight. We want to see the glory of Lord, the throne of God, and the way of Jesus Christ. We should be able to discern Lord's way from the corrupt way of the world. We need our spiritual sight open and our hearts' desires renewed to be able to discern his way to God's kingdom.

The Contents of the Right Living

Our pursuits or the contents of our living should be different in order to walk on the right path. The right purpose is a prerequisite of the right direction. The followers of Balaam pursued the following. "These are wells without water, clouds carried by a tempest, for whom is reserved the blackness of darkness forever. For when they speak great swelling words of emptiness, they allure through the lusts of the flesh, through lewdness, the ones who have actually escaped from those who live in error" (2 Pet 2:17–18).

"Wells without water" describes a double-sided reality of life, full of lies and trickery. Water is scarce in the Middle East. Imagine this. A traveler was crossing a desert. He saw a well and ran to it. But the well was empty.

Unlike a decent outer appearance, a life may be missing living water. "Clouds carried by a tempest" is another analogy. Some versions of the Bible record "clouds" as "fog" as well. Take notice that these are not just any clouds. They are carried by a tempest. Usually, such clouds should be accompanied by thunder, lightning, or showers of rain. But these empty clouds are loud without rain. They symbolized the false living of false teachers and prophets. Their outer appearances did not match the substance inside.

Let us humbly re-examine our churches. Are they lacking the real substance, the gospel, while they appear presentable with many programs? Are they missing Jesus while they are loud on the outside? Our churches should have marks of true Christians and a true church.

The followers of Balaam "spoke great swelling words of emptiness." Since they bragged about the outer shells, their words were only empty. With their empty words, they still "allured through the lusts of the flesh, through lewdness." This was typical of Balaam's doing. He went to curse the Israelites, but he couldn't do it. God intervened in that situation. Eventually Balaam went up to the high places of Baal where he could observe the extent of the Israelites. He ended up blessing them instead of cursing. King Balak took Balaam to another place to see if they can still curse part of Israel. But the same thing happened. It actually repeated three times and King Balak became angry. He had paid Balaam a handsome amount of materials to curse Israel, yet Balaam could only bless Israel. Then Balaam realized that it was impossible to curse Israel and shared a secret to lead Israel to its demise. The secret trick was having the Moabite women seduce the Israelite men. Israelite men, then, would participate in worshiping the gods of Moab. In the ancient days, worship services by the gentiles often involved sexual relations of the worshipers. The Lord's anger blazed against his people, and a plague swept them.

This is the way of Balaam. It destroys and kills others as well as oneself. Balaam was put to death after he drove the Israelites into the fire of Lord's rage. The way of Balaam brings destruction to others and oneself. Has God called us to be destroyed? No. He called us so we could live and let others live, too. God called Abraham to be a passage of blessings for all the nations. We are Abraham's spiritual descendants. Christians not only save their own lives but also share them with others so they can be saved too. This would be the right model to emulate for Christians. We only live once. What kind of influence are you making? What kind of fruits are you leaving behind? We should share God's living water and blessings with others. God's purpose of calling us is this.

Let me share a story of Tae-seob Choi. He was an elder at church and a founder of a company called Korea Glass Industry Co., Ltd. He was originally from North Korea and worked many rough jobs. He delivered milk and worked as an assistant in an auto body shop. While making a living was tough, he always kept a mindset of living the faith right.

He finally got a loan and started a small business. Shortly after, the Korean War (also known as "625") broke. People in Seoul, South Korea, had to flee. But CEO Choi went to a bank to repay all of his loan. A bank employee was surprised that anyone would repay his loan, not cling to it at a time like this. "Are you sure you want to pay it back? You know that we are in war, and honestly I don't even know where the record book is. So it's not necessary to do this now." But CEO Choi insisted on paying it back, regardless of the records. He handed over his bag of money and requested a receipt. The bank employee had to write a receipt with his signature stamp on it.

How can we understand this? The bank documents could have been lost or displaced. When lives were on the line, who would even care about paying back loans in war? Frankly honesty doesn't guarantee good rewards.

However, CEO Choi lived his faith even during the war. After the war ended, he started a business on Jeju Island. He needed a fishing ship, so he went to the bank to apply for a loan. Without any cash or collateral, the bank would not give out a loan. He, too, got rejected. But on the way out, he showed that receipt as the last straw. The bank officer was delighted to see it. "You are him. I heard your story. You paid back the loan even during the war." He was a legend in the banking industry. The officer assessed that the normal rules could be relaxed for a legend like him, even if the current conditions were not met. He proceeded to arrange a meeting with the head of the branch and a loan was approved. That started a small business, which later grew to be Korea Glass Industry Co., Ltd.

While all this was truly impressive and touching, I found one more treasure in his story. CEO Choi donated all of his wealth to society upon death. He was known to found a philanthropic organization to support the hungry in Africa when he was living. He spent his money for the kingdom of God and donated all of the remainder when he left this world. I feel very proud of the fact that an exemplary Christian like CEO Choi lived in Korea. If we have only one person like this, we have hope in Korea.

Many people feel pessimistic about Korean society and lament the dark and confused reality. But Korean society didn't get dark due to the world, as the world has always been corrupt. The politics of this world have always been unclean. It's not on them that Korea declined recently. Rather, it is on compromising Christians who left God's way and chose the corrupt Balaam's way. Hope in Korean society also evaporated. Unless we return to the right way, Korea is hopeless. Unless we return to the path of faith, Korean will not recover. They say Korea has become an economic power, but Korea cannot be used by God unless it straightens its path.

We only live once. The world may push us to hurry our ways and become the best at what we do, regardless of the method. But if we choose their way, the way of Balaam, hope will be gone.

We must stick to the right way. Jesus showed the right way. The way of carrying the cross is his way, not pursuing the glory of the world. Humanity was saved because of the sacrificial death of Jesus on the cross. We should also follow his way so the rest of the world in suffering and pain can be saved. Hope will be found then. The glory of his kingdom will be restored.

REPLACING CYNICISM WITH LOVE

> [1] A prophecy: The word of the Lord to Israel through Malachi.
> [2] "I have loved you," says the LORD.
> "But you ask, 'How have you loved us?'
> "Was not Esau Jacob's brother?" declares the LORD. "Yet I have loved Jacob, [3] but Esau I have hated, and I have turned his hill country into a wasteland and left his inheritance to the desert jackals."
> [4] Edom may say, "Though we have been crushed, we will rebuild the ruins."
> But this is what the Lord Almighty says: "They may build, but I will demolish. They will be called the Wicked Land, a people always under the wrath of the Lord. [5] You will see it with your own eyes and say, 'Great is the Lord—even beyond the borders of Israel!'" (Mal 1:1–5)

The origin of the word "cynicism" is from the Cynics of ancient Greece, a school of thought. Their academic style was to pursue a life matching nature. However, the cynicism of today came to have a more criticizing and pessimistic attitude towards reality. This was well-described as "nihilism behind a smile" by Wim Rietkerk in his book *If Only I Could Believe*. On the outside they smile, but on the inside their hearts feel empty. Behind a smile, coldness and crookedness exist. They react negatively to just about anything as uncaring spectators. "Try all you can. Just don't involve me. I already tried enough. I'm sure it won't work out." After hearing a long story, they just sneer, saying "So what?" like a typical cynic. Cynicism is dangerous because it takes away passion. The direction of life will follow after the negative and crooked heart. The flip side of cynicism is distrust. People become cynical when they cannot trust society and politicians. Similarly, they become cynical towards people and love when they cannot trust them.

Korean society of today is filled with distrust. Especially towards politics, the degree of distrust is through the roof. Let me share a joke about Korean politics. If someone runs for a position in congress and wins, they will be surprised three times. First, they are surprised at "how a person like me gets appointed." Second, once they enter congress, they see that the majority of congresspeople are just like themselves. Thirdly, they are surprised by "how a country still is being run by people like them." Additionally, they are surprised when the people still trust what they say, when they don't trust it themselves.

What is even more dangerous is that this kind of deep distrust towards society, politics, or interpersonal relations is a distrusting attitude towards God. When we distrust his words, covenants, and love, it can dissolve our lives. So many Christians are trapped in this distrusting cynicism and live on without the passion of faith. They reluctantly come to church and sit through the service habitually. Their hearts are not truly moved or touched in the worship. They come close to the surface of faith yet only stay outside. They are unable to step further into the world of faith. When this gets worse, they could leave God and the church.

These people with the mindset of cynicism might look for causes of something outside of themselves. For example, they argue that their hearts toward God got cold and cynical due to many disappointing practices of church. Yes, as many acknowledge, churches of today have become very secularized. Understandably some people may get disappointed at materialistic and corrupt churches and close their hearts. Also, they may stumble due to other church members. For example, they see a good member who served church well fall into temptation overnight. We cannot deny the above factors contribute to the external causes that block God from these cynical people.

But the most fundamental reason for their spiritual cynicism lies in their personal relationships with God. In the right knowledge and relationship with God, we cannot fall into cynicism. Broken relationships with God lead to cynicism. When was religion ever not corrupt? Was there any church in the past that was flawlessly clean and holy? Were the Israelites of the Old Testament all holy? Can we say that they were more holy than the Christians of today? Was the religion of the Jesus' days clean? A corrupt church thus cannot be enough basis for justifying one's spiritual cynicism. Let us take David as an example, if other members of church test you. Once a king of a nation and a giant of faith, how did he collapse? He committed terrible sins such as adultery and murder (organizing and instigating it). Was it right that the entire Israel decided to leave God because of David's fallacies?

Although external factors influence us, the more fundamental reason for cynicism lies within our relationships with God. The right relationship with him will enable us to overcome any environmental or people-related challenges. No matter how long you have attended church, if you keep a distance from God and do not enter into a deeper relationship with him, you will miss out on him.

God's Love Overcomes Cynicism

God gave a warning through the prophet Malachi to the Israelites about cynicism. A "warning" in the ancient days was more of an "oracle," a proclamation of judgment. The warning from God's prophet was analogous to a preview of the upcoming judgment of God. Malachi is the last book of the Old Testament. It was recorded in 420 B.C., and it was the last message of prophecy from God before the return of Messiah. This was about one hundred years after Zerubbabel had completed building a temple.

The Israelites returned to their homeland after their captivity in Babylon. They saw that it was in ruins. There was little food due to famine. The survival was tough. However, God told Zerubbabel to build a temple. The people hesitated, so God sent more prophets such as Haggai and Zechariah to proclaim his vision. Although things were in shame and pain at present, Jerusalem was going to be restored after the temple was completed. God's glory was going to return, and Israel was going to be the center of all the nations once again. The people listened and dedicated to building the temple. They gave offerings when they couldn't eat well. This way the temple became completed.

Then did the promised prosperity return to them? Nothing happened after ten years, then twenty years. A few generations changed, yet nothing happened. Even after one hundred years of continued hardship and pressures from other countries, there was no hope in sight. It only became harder as they gave up on the hope of a better future.

It would be natural to feel that faith in God was useless in their shoes. If obedience to his words brought no glory, one might conclude that faith was useless. We can conjecture that such distrust kept accumulating in their hearts in the day of Malachi. When God expressed love, their reaction was indifferent.

"I have loved you, says the Lord. But you ask, 'How have you loved us?'" (Mal 1:2). This would be similar to our response of saying "Really?" to someone who confesses his or her love. It's a show of distrust. They questioned his love because their suffering didn't cease. They assumed that their faith in God would make him take away their suffering and hardships. They thought that the loveless God abandoned them to their problems.

It's common that Christians cling to God first when they face a problem. They anticipate his coming to rescue, if they serve at church faithfully. They try to endure in church fellowships. But other members of church poke at their fragile hearts. Eventually they even leave church due to the hurts. Almost no one would be exempt from having suffered some sort of disappointments and hurts from God and church. We should still overcome it. We cannot experience God deeply if we stay in the shallow cynicism, fed by unrealized expectations and resolutions of our problems. They cannot coexist. If you commit to follow Jesus yet keep a deep-seated cynicism, your life will not be fulfilled. We cannot live a life pleasing to him and worthy of his glory if our hearts remain bitter and untrusting. We will waste our lives. Instead we must rise above the cynicism. We must know God's love well to rise above. Let us look at his love in three aspects.

Have a Conviction in God's Love

We need to know the essence of God's love to rise above cynicism. When we truly experience God's love, we can overcome the pain of the environment. Most problems we encounter with faith boil down to the issue of our conviction in God's love. We are not certain of his love. Without a conviction, we cannot conquer our problems.

God refuted the Israelites in regards to their cynicism. "'Was not Esau Jacob's brother?' declares the Lord; 'Yet I have loved Jacob, but Esau I have hated, and I have turned his hill country into a wasteland and left his inheritance to the desert jackals.'" The reason he brought up the story of Esau and Jacob was to illustrate the essence of his love. Esau and Jacob were born twins. From the moment of birth, they competed, and Jacob came out second by just a few seconds. But God loved Jacob more.

Apostle Paul witnessed that God loved Jacob more since he was in the womb of Rebecca. It might be easier to understand if someone favored one twin to another after he or she saw their actual behaviors after birth. But God already chose and favored Jacob prenatally. It explains the unconditional aspect of his love. He doesn't love based on our deeds or performance scores. Unconditionally he already chose and loved us.

If the Israelites didn't realize this, they would never be able to return to God. He didn't choose Israel for their superior qualities over other nations. It was an unconditional, one-way decision of God. This is the heart of his love. Were any of us chosen by God based on our talents? No one was. We were all sinners yet God loved us. "This is love: not that we loved God, but that he loved us and sent his Son as an atoning sacrifice for our sins" (1 John 4:10). God initiated. He approached us first and gave his Son as an atoning sacrifice. He did when we were completely unqualified. With this understanding, we should be only grateful. We might also be apologetic. While we are such wretched sinners, how can his love so great? A true spiritual journey begins when we are grateful and overwhelmed with his unconditional love.

Peter ironically came to truly understand God's love after his big failure. Peter was called and lived as a disciple of Jesus. But at the time of Jesus' arrest, Peter failed to defend him. He even denied Jesus three times, right in front of his face. It was a true betrayal and failure. It also wounded him at a deep level. He probably thought that this was absolutely the end. He wouldn't be able to have anything more to do with Jesus. Actually he left everything and went to the Tiberias beach. He returned to being a fisherman like before. But when he thought that he passed the point of no return, Jesus came to see him. He asked the empty-handed Peter, "Do you love me?" He asked three times in total. Peter, the betrayer, responded, "You know that I love you." Then Jesus commissioned him to feed the lambs. Peter's recovery began.

God comes to us when we are at the absolute bottom. If we remember the moment of his special grace in times of our troubles, we can run the race for him for the rest of our lives. Peter was executed upside down on a cross. Until that moment, he committed to living for Jesus. We all need this personal experience of his love. If we hold onto his great love, we can rise above any circumstances and run our race for him.

Live God's Love

After we understand the essence of his love, we need to *experience* it. In other words, we need to feel and live his love beyond theory and notion. His love is not abstract. It's very real. It's breathing and living in our very lives.

God poured tangible grace unto Israel, beyond empty words. He made the enemy of Israel, Edom, desolate and left their inheritance to the desert jackals. "They may build, but I will demolish. They will be called the Wicked Land, a people always under the wrath of the Lord" (Mal 1:4).

God was in rage against Edom's descendants as well (Edom was a descendant of Esau). The word "edom" meant "red" and it was a nickname of Esau. God said he would demolish Edom's hill country and drive them into the desert. If they gathered strength and rebuilt the ruins, God said to tear them down again and make them uninhabitable. We might think God is excessive. Would it be really necessary to stay enraged forever? But consider that the descendants of Jacob and those of Esau were at odds, not only from a blood-relation standpoint but also from a spiritual standpoint. The descendants of Jacob represented God's people, while those of Esau represented the anti-Christ that opposed God. The competition between Jacob and Esau actually extended to the competition between God's people and their enemy.

Actually the first people who blocked the way of Israelites who were about to enter the Canaan land were Edom's descendants. They were the biggest obstacle before the promised land. Even afterward the descendants of Edom stayed resentful towards the Israelites and they rejoiced when Israelites ran into trouble. It wasn't a simple hate but a deep-rooted resentment. In 586 B.C. the Southern Kingdom, Judah, was destroyed by Babylon, and the temple of Jerusalem was set on fire. The descendants of Edom were joyous, clapping their hands. They supported Babylon, not their own brother, on the worst day of judgment in the Judah's history. They assisted Babylon in capturing the Jerusalem castle and the Judah people.

This was such a betrayal and treason in the history of Israel. As if this was not bad enough, Edom's people came to occupy the land that was previously inhabited by the Judah people. As they lived, mixing with the remainders of Judah, a new ethnic group called "Idumaean" emerged. The most famous person of the Idumaeans is the Herod the Great. Herod was the appointed king of the whole of Judea by the Roman Empire, but he was not a pure Jew, as he was of the mixed Idumaean. This is why he was wildly shocked when the three wise men broke the news of the birth of the king of the Jews. He knew that he lacked the direct lineage by blood. If the news were true, the newborn king would threaten his throne. Out of his fear and insecurity, he ordered all the babies under two years to be killed in that region. This was such a barbaric and unprecedentedly evil crime. Herod is still remembered as a Satanic figure to this day. It's the most outrageous and terrible sin to oppose God and block the Messiah as a human being. The fact that Herod was a descendant of Edom was not a mere coincidence. Edom opposed Israel, God's nation, and tried to kill baby Jesus.

Because Edom opposed and made Israelites suffer, God promised to demolish them in his time. He gave his word of his judgment of the eventual demise of Edom as a consequence of their sin. This is God's love. He's not looking down on us from far away. He is hands-on in our lives. He doesn't just talk the talk of loving us. Instead he actually helps, protects, and even deals with our enemies. "In all things God works for the good of those who love him" (Rom 8:28). This is the realistic and practical aspect of his love. We can lean on him to get through our difficult problems for his love is practical.

Let me share an episode from a book, *Happy to Be Able to Cry with Someone Who is Crying*, written by Jeong-ok Yu (she is wife of Pastor Young-do Lee at Seoul Hanaro Church). It was about her son, having been raised in Christian family with faith. He had graduated from college and entered the mandatory military service. Unfortunately he was under a terrible senior. The senior knew about his asthma and gave him a hard time. Before breakfast time in the morning, he would make her son run around the training field, fully armored. Already bad enough for regular soldiers, this was such an ordeal for someone with asthma. He couldn't even swallow food well after. But they didn't wait for him to finish. They put away food when time was up.

He shared this story with his mother on his leave. We can only imagine how it made her heart ache. Although she probably felt so bad, she advised her son in faith. "No matter what, do not oppose him. Obey him in your faith for God. I cannot do anything for you, but I promise to pray for you at that morning hour of your rounds." And she did pray every morning for him after he went back.

Two months later she received a letter from her son. The first opening word was "Hallelujah." It was good news. The daily morning training healed his asthma. The rough routine must have strengthened his immunity, and he no longer had asthma symptoms. Her son cried for joy as he ran. He was so grateful for God's grace. He even went up to the senior and thanked him: "You helped cure my asthma. I'm really grateful." The senior probably felt ashamed and uneasy. He changed his attitude and didn't give him a hard time again.

God's love is not abstract. He is hands-on with our practical problems. He carries out solutions in a real and specific way. If we lean on the almighty God, his love helps us overcome obstacles in any life's situations. We can get back up and run in any circumstances because of his love. Let us remember his unconditional love is practical. God's love is real.

See the Vision of God's Love

We have to see the vision of God's love in order to rise above faith stained with cynicism. If we can see the dream and vision of the future through God's love, we can overcome dark reality. Eventually the cynical Israelites will see with their eyes who God is. They will exclaim and shout, "The Lord is a great even beyond the borders of Israel!" This means his name will be proclaimed to all nations beyond Israel. It contains a declarative message of the Messiah's vision that he will come to save us. Although the present reality may be dark and frustrating, the Messiah will come to our land, and all nations will come to God. This kind of vision will surely give us strength to get through the present hardships.

When do we get disappointed in God? When we get disappointed, would our disappointments be nearly comparable to the complete dismay that the apostles of Jesus had felt upon his crucifixion? They followed Jesus for three years. They left everything behind and committed wholly to him. They learned under Jesus, went where he sent them, and survived sea storms and wilderness with him. They followed him with the dream and vision of his kingdom to come. Then they had to watch Jesus get arrested and crucified. It must have been crushing. Perhaps they felt that all their efforts and sacrifices had been for nothing.

So they went into hiding. They were devastatingly disappointed. They lost hope. But three days after the crucifixion, human history changed forever. Little did they know that God's grand plan of saving humanity was completed on the cross. Had they known this, they wouldn't have gone into hiding. The glory of resurrection awaited. Heaven was going to open, and the Holy Spirt was going to pour down on the heads of all his disciples. After this, the disciples of Jesus, filled with the Holy Spirit, were going to be witnesses to all nations to the ends of the earth. It was the vision of the cross.

We are just like them. Let us not be mistaken and complain that God doesn't do anything on our behalf. God is always working. It's just that we don't see everything, but God is working in his mysterious ways. His works enrich our lives and make them more beautiful. They will bring new blessings at a higher level. Thus, we have to trust in God's love, his works, and his vision.

Let us drop the pessimistic, negative, and cynical attitude. Instead let us be restored with fervent faith. God never abandons us. Sometimes we grow apart from God. God never ceases to love us. He is always there. Sometimes we turn our backs to God, when the going gets tough in life. God still loves us. There is no one free of hurt. Sometimes we get emotionally wounded at church or on our walks in faith in life. Sometimes we misbelieve that God abandoned us. Our hearts may have turned calloused and cynical. I sincerely encourage you to give our hurts to God and run to his arms.

GOD'S TOUCH

> [1] So in the ninth year of Zedekiah's reign, on the tenth day of the tenth month, Nebuchadnezzar king of Babylon marched against Jerusalem with his whole army. He encamped outside the city and built siege works all around it. [2] The city was kept under siege until the eleventh year of King Zedekiah.
> [3] By the ninth day of the fourth month the famine in the city had become so severe that there was no food for the people to eat. [4] Then the city wall was broken through, and the whole army fled at night through the gate between the two walls near the king's garden, though the Babylonians were surrounding the city. They fled toward the Arabah, [5] but the Babylonian army pursued the king and overtook him in the plains of Jericho. All his soldiers were separated from him and scattered, [6] and he was captured.

He was taken to the king of Babylon at Riblah, where sentence was pronounced on him. [7] They killed the sons of Zedekiah before his eyes. Then they put out his eyes, bound him with bronze shackles and took him to Babylon.
[8] On the seventh day of the fifth month, in the nineteenth year of Nebuchadnezzar king of Babylon, Nebuzaradan commander of the imperial guard, an official of the king of Babylon, came to Jerusalem. [9] He set fire to the temple of the Lord, the royal palace and all the houses of Jerusalem. Every important building he burned down. [10] The whole Babylonian army under the commander of the imperial guard broke down the walls around Jerusalem. [11] Nebuzaradan the commander of the guard carried into exile the people who remained in the city, along with the rest of the populace and those who had deserted to the king of Babylon. [12] But the commander left behind some of the poorest people of the land to work the vineyards and fields. (2 Kgs 25:1–12)

When we want to treat a physical illness, we need to find a good doctor who will give the right diagnosis and prescription. The right combination of these will put us on the right track for recovery. However, an incorrect diagnosis will lead to a wrong prescription, then make even an easy-to-treat illness very difficult. These days giving the right diagnosis has become quite difficult because patients have become too informed. People often do some research on their symptoms on the internet, and some come prepared with their own diagnoses, which then will only need a doctor's signing off on a prescription. Is it alright for a patient to self-diagnosis? A diagnosis should be left to a medical professional. Then the right prescription and right treatment will be possible.

The same goes for our problems in life. Our problems come in a variety of forms. Some are physical and some are spiritual, as they arise from a broken and damaged soul. The most serious problem of these would be our sin. This disease called sin is not readily visible, as it is deeply hidden inside our souls and spirits. But this disease makes our souls and spirits get very sick to become like untreated wounds with puss. When this happens, we cannot go to just anyone. We have to find the right healer who knows our spirits well and can diagnose correctly.

Only one healer can do that, and that is our God. He created us, so he knows us well. He knows us in all aspects: in our body, spirit, and mind. He is also the almighty God. So he can heal us from any disease. Thus, when we struggle with problems, we should come to him. Let us seek and receive his prescription to be healed.

God's Prescription

The last two chapters in 2 Kings record the last days that followed the reign of King Josiah. King Josiah was the last good king of Judah. After he got killed at Megiddo, the kingdom of Judah rapidly declined. We can imagine how chaotic and disorderly it was while they changed their king four times during twenty-three years. After the death of King Josiah, his son, Jehoahaz, succeeded the throne. Only three months after, he got killed by an Egyptian king. Then his brother, Jehoiakim, became the next king, but he lasted eleven years until he was captured by Babylon. His son, Jehoiachin, followed his suit, but only after three months, he was captured by Babylon as well.

The last king was Zedekiah. He is known to be an uncle of Jehoiachin, making him a son of King Josiah. Zedekiah the King saw with his own eyes the fates that befell the prior three kings in the last eleven years. They all played political games against Babylon and ended up becoming captives. Judah fell into ruins. Additionally, the prophet Jeremiah, God's faithful servant, had proclaimed his message to them. They should have listened and returned to God. But Zedekiah did not turn back. He left God, kept on committing evil acts and only sought to find political solutions.

As a consequence, in 588 B.C., his ninth year, Babylon invaded again. King Nebuchadnezzar of Babylon executed a full-fledged attack with a great army. They climbed up to Jerusalem and on all four sides built a clay fortress. This period of besieging was two years. In the ancient days, those that were trapped inside a fortress would face hardships at all levels. They would run out of food and water eventually. The famine and hunger would continue. To make matters worse, the ruler made an escape hole during the night and ran away to save himself. The solders of Babylon spotted him and captured him. The sons of Zedekiah got killed, and Zedekiah became a prisoner of war with his eyes removed by them. The misery didn't end with him. Jerusalem also fell to the ground.

Judah was a God-ruling kingdom. How could such a kingdom be devastated like that? Some explain it with international relations of that period. Egypt of the south and Babylon of the north were at battle. Then as Babylon won in 605 B.C., Judah became a scapegoat between the two. But a more fundamental cause would be found in their relationship with God. God sent a prophet to give them multiple warnings. Judah still didn't turn back from its evil ways. It remained deeply immersed in its sinful ways. Like a spring that got too overstretched to return to its original length, Judah could not return to God.

Interestingly Judah's sin was evident from an objective perspective, but they themselves did not realize it. Their inside was already damaged beyond repair, yet Zedekiah didn't realize it and kept playing political games among nations. It had reached an unrecoverable state, so God gave an extreme prescription of his judgment through Babylon.

It was not a simple coincidence when God used Babylon to judge Judah. It was the only way to revive Judah. His intent was not to destroy Judah. Rather, he planned to restore it, making it depart from sin and purify itself.

In our eyes God's judgment may appear too harsh. But let us remember that his disciplining us is not meant to condemn us. He loves us, and sometimes that is the only way to bring us back to healing. Thus, when our lives have problems, we should receive God's prescriptions. Come to God before people or this world and take his prescriptions. Then our lives, no matter how irreparable they seem, will be renewed.

Step 1: Cutting Out a Wound

The first step in God's treatment plan is to remove the wounded area. If we cover up a wound, we cannot treat it properly. We need to identify the root cause and remove it to bring recovery.

The Southern Judah was in a dire state beyond repair. Dethroning the king and sending the people as prisoners would not be a solution to the fundamental problem Judah faced. The root cause actually lay within Judah's people. So God executed his special treatment plan. It occurred on the seventh day of the fifth month of the nineteenth year of King Nebuchadnezzar's reign in Babylon. This translated to fall on the seventh day of the fifth month in 586 B.C. The fifth month on the Judah calendar corresponds to July or August of the modern calendar we use. The prophet Jeremiah said this day was the tenth. After rabbis adjusted this date to the ninth in the period of diaspora, it is being observed as the day of the siege of Jerusalem to this day.

The reason why the Jews observe this day is that the Babylon troops burned down the temple of the Lord, the royal palace, and all the houses in Jerusalem. The holy temple was burned down. This is shocking news to us today. Imagine how the Jews must have been in utter shock. They probably asked how God could allow such an atrocity to them, God's chosen people. How could he allow his own people to be trampled by the gentiles and his sanctuary to be burned down? Actually this was the hardest part they could not wrap their heads around. In their time, the Jewish people believed that a solid sanctuary guaranteed protection of its people. They blindly believed that the holy temple made them invincible. So they worshiped the holy temple. Whether Assyria or Babylon invaded them, whether they continued to commit sin, they thought God would still protect them. Then the holy temple was burned down.

The holy temple was at the core of their religion. It was the center of Jewish spirituality. At the heart of the Jewish lives were the worshiping and sacrificing ceremonies. So what more could have been left after the holy temple burned to the ground? Judah misbelieved because they thought the holy temple was the building. If they kept the physical building intact, they thought God would protect them. But the truth was that God's presence gave the building its meaning. Take Solomon's temple for example. He built it with utmost extravagance and beauty. Every pillar was covered with gold and decorated with shining treasures. But regardless of its glorious appearance, if God wasn't present, then it would no longer be a true temple.

Among the sins committed by the kings of Judah, defiling the sanctuary by permitting idolatry inside the temple is considered to be the most evil one. Manasseh is considered the most evil king, and he "erected altars to Baal and made an Asherah pole . . . He bowed down to all the starry hosts and worshipped them" (2 Kgs 21:3). On the outside it pretended to be the holy temple, yet it was full of detestable sins. It was only an empty shell.

In Jesus' time, it was also at the sanctuary where the most detestable abominations were committed by Jewish religious leaders. Inside the sanctuary, merchants were depriving poor people. The so-called religious leaders were taking profits off of the market activity. The supposedly most holy place had become a sinful and unclean marketplace.

God knew this spiritual irony, as he was not fooled by our outer appearance. God saw through the inside. So he cut out the evil sin from Judah's center of religion, the holy temple. He burned down the temple through Babylon's troops.

God wants to see his presence and holiness in our spirits. Do we truly have a temple, a place of worship in our hearts? If so, God will accept us. Our worships need to be truthfully alive, and we need God to be present. It will be futile to acknowledge God by mouth when our hearts are in contradiction. What use would empty religious activities without God be? They would not please God.

Korean churches need to re-examine themselves for the above reason. The outer shell such as appearance and size bears no importance or meaning to God. He cares about the inside. Let us re-examine the center of our hearts. If we have sinned, we should surrender our sins to the blood of the cross and ask for forgiveness. Then we can be renewed. Cutting out our sinful wound is the first step in God's treatment.

Step 2: Putting Us through Refining Fire

The second step in God's treatment plan is to put us through refining fire. Suffering for the Jews didn't stop after the holy temple was burned down. God allowed Babylonian troops to loot the Jews. They tore down the four walls of the fortress and took the remaining people of the fortress as captives. Babylon did this three times. The first time was when they captured many young Jewish people in 605 B.C. during the reign of King Jehoiakim. Among them were Daniel and his three friends. The second time was when they took many leaders and influential people along with King Jehoiachin in 597 B.C. The prophet Ezekiel was among them. The third time was when they took most of the Jews of Jerusalem, except the lowest class, in 586 B.C.

The captive period in Babylon was a time of suffering and hardships for the Jewish people. They lost the sovereignty of their nation and their land. They got taken as prisoners of war to a foreign land. On the outside, this was the darkest and most disgraceful time in their history. But God purified them during this period. The seventy-year period of captivity was a blessing in disguise, as he was removing their impurities to rebuild them.

Actually, the Jews initiated work that was never done before. First, they started to gather God's laws in fragments, then organize them with a new perspective. A product of this effort became the Old Testament as we know it today. Among the captives were many priests and Levites. The respected religious leaders of Judah could not help but ask themselves why the Jews had fallen so miserably. Then they found the reason. They realized that they did not obey God's words. So they started a revival movement to go back to the laws.

Also, the Jews started to worship at synagogues during their captivity. A synagogue was a type of an educational institute that reinforced teaching the next generations of Israel about the faith of their ancestors. It also connected various organizations and acted as a spiritual center. On gentile lands, they taught the laws to children on the Sabbath days. This tradition has survived to the present day. We see that synagogues are still found at the center of the Jewish communities everywhere in the world. The synagogue served to preserve the identity of the scattered Jews over thousands of years. The Jews advanced their belief in the coming Messiah during this time. Their exile made them look towards the recovery and rebuilding of the Jews as well as the everlasting kingdom of God. They developed a firm theology in the Messiah's deliverance. So the period of suffering was beneficial rather than wasteful. It served as refining fire that purified and renewed their spirituality.

If we can relate our current situations to a hot and painful furnace, let us ponder God's intent behind this. We may complain and resent initially. But let us remember God's reason. He wants to purify our faith to the next level.

Attending church doesn't guarantee pure faith. Not all gold is the same. It comes in different grades of purity. To achieve a 99.9 percent purity for a gold bar, it needs twenty repetitions of a purifying process in the hot furnace. Passing through the very painful process, we attain a clean and purified soul. If we are diligently participating in many ministries at church, we actually need to check the purity of our faith more. A higher degree of purity enables us to know God more deeply and hear him. The more pure our faith is, the deeper we can experience God's works.

I heard a testimony of a church member living in Dallas, Texas. He owned a clothing store. The business wasn't doing well, so he moved to Oklahoma. Compared to Dallas, Oklahoma's situation was even worse. It was a more desolate place where the Korean population size was smaller. Making a living was tough, and the business environment was challenging. Somehow all this motivated him to make a determination to take a stab at running a business like a true Christian. So he made four principles to himself and kept them. First, he threw out all the knockoffs and fake products. People in the fashion industry would be well aware of how lucrative this market was. But he got rid of them all. Second, he closed business on Sundays. He declared it as the Sabbath, the Lord's Day. Thirdly, he paid every single cent of tax. This also was not easy for a businessman, but to keep integrity as a faithful Christian, he did. Fourth, he always gave a tithe, a tenth of his earnings. In short, he firmly decided to take the unprofitable path. Following these principles, making income was hard and so was making a living.

One day he was on his way to a wholesale market to purchase items. It was raining. To avoid getting wet, he went under a shade in front of a store, and he noticed a piece of apparel in the display. It grabbed his attention, so he bought some clothes from there instead of the original store he had in mind. This clothing item became a best seller at his store, and it catapulted his business to the next level.

One day he received an offer from a big apparel business. It was a good opportunity to sell his merchandise and grow the business. But after the first meeting, the offer was withdrawn. He talked so honestly that his projections of business growth and revenue size didn't meet their expectation. But he received a call the next day. An executive from that company wanted to see him again, saying "Frankly I'm not attracted to your clothing lines, but I was impressed with your honesty." Eventually they signed a contract because the executive highly regarded and trusted his ethics. After this big contract was won, he produced and sold mass volumes. His business grew successfully and became the business that gave the most tithes in the states of Texas and Oklahoma.

The secret to success is not out of reach. Pure faith opened his eyes to see God's guidance, which led to success in business in this case. These days many people blame the environment. They complain about hostile living conditions. Let us have complete faith in God. We will overcome any challenges. After God removes our wounded area, we need to go through a purification process.

Step 3: New Recovery

The last step in God's treatment plan is a new recovery. God allowed Jerusalem to fall to the ground as his judgment to the Jews. He gave a time of suffering to purify them during their captivity. But it didn't end there. He also prepared a new drama. He didn't mean for the ending to be despair. They say they can tell by the last scene of a movie whether its sequel will come out. The last verse in 2 Kings is a preview of the next sequel that God prepared. "In the thirty-seventh year of the exile of Jehoiachin king of Judah, in the year Awel-Marduk became king of Babylon, he released Jehoiachin king of Judah from prison. He did this on the twenty-seventh day of the twelfth month. He spoke kindly to him and gave him a seat of honor higher than those of the other kings who were with him in Babylon. So Jehoiachin put aside his prison clothes and for the rest of his life ate regularly at the king's table. Day by day the king gave Jehoiachin a regular allowance as long as he lived" (2 Kgs 25:27–30).

Jehoiachin was the last descendant in King David's lineage, and was taken to Babylon as prisoner of war. He got released after thirty-seven years in prison. The king of Babylon restored his status as king and provided enough food and clothes. Along with King Jehoiachin, the Jews embraced a new chapter. Thirty years after, the grandson of Jehoiachin, Zerubbabel, brought back about fifty thousand Jewish people and rebuilt the holy temple.

God started a new chapter in history. Judah had fallen, and David's heritage seemed to be over. Yet God released Jehoiachin and returned his grandson to rewrite the future of Judah. On their lost land, they began to rebuild a temple and his kingdom. Ultimately God's big plan was to fulfill the vision of his kingdom through Jesus Christ, who came as David's descendant. When man is at a dead end, then God starts working. God already prepared, long in advance, a meticulous plan to restore the Jews from their captivity and transform them to be truly God's people. It is God's amazing plan.

God foretold through the prophet Jeremiah, "This is what the Lord says: 'When seventy years are completed for Babylon, I will come to you and fulfill my good promise to bring you back to this place. For I know the plans I have for you,' declares the Lord, "plans to prosper you and not to harm you, plans to give you hope and a future. Then you will call on me and come and pray to me, and I will listen to you. You will seek me and find me when you seek me with all your heart'" (Jer 29:10–13).

It was inevitable that the Jews had to pay the consequences of their sin as captives, but God said they would be released after seventy years. God intended peace and hope for the future of the Jews. His treatment plan was to purify the Jews and give them peace. So before lamenting our hardships or failures, let us remember messianic hope.

God wants to restore a broken relationship with his people. He wants to open again a door of prayer that was closed. He wants to open a window to heaven. Even when God seemed to leave the Jews completely, he came and promised them a new hope and recovery. We all need God. No matter what problems befall us, the moment God intervenes, they will all be resolved. He is the clue. The reason for the fall and recovery of the Jews was God.

God is the only one who can restore and transform our lives. I encourage you to meet him personally and fulfill his will in your life with his presence. No one is without problems. No life is without crises. It's useless to seek solutions from people. The only solution is God. He will give us strength. We will embrace a blessed new day in his presence.

RECOVERY OF A BROKEN LIFE

> [1] "Put the trumpet to your lips!
>   An eagle is over the house of the Lord
> because the people have broken my covenant
>   and rebelled against my law.
> [2] Israel cries out to me,
>   'Our God, we acknowledge you!'
> [3] But Israel has rejected what is good;
>   an enemy will pursue him.
> [4] They set up kings without my consent;
>   they choose princes without my approval.
> With their silver and gold
>   they make idols for themselves
>   to their own destruction.
> [5] Samaria, throw out your calf-idol!
>   My anger burns against them.
> How long will they be incapable of purity?
> [6]   They are from Israel!
> This calf—a metalworker has made it;
>   it is not God.
> It will be broken in pieces,
>   that calf of Samaria.
> [7] "They sow the wind
>   and reap the whirlwind.
> The stalk has no head;
>   it will produce no flour.
> Were it to yield grain,
>   foreigners would swallow it up.
> [8] Israel is swallowed up;
>   now she is among the nations
>   like something no one wants." (Hos 8:1–8)

Reginald Howard White was a famous American professional football player who had a very successful career. He played for the Green Bay

Packers for six years and won a Super Bowl championship. His story was in the book *Failing Forward*. He was serving as an assistant minister of a Baptist church in Tennessee while he played football. At an interview with sports magazine reporters, he was asked, "What is your secret to becoming a talented football player?" White responded, "It's all because of my excellent coach. He taught me how to fall when I began playing."

Generally they teach how to penetrate the opponent's defense and score a goal. But White said he first learned how to fall. His knees got bruised and bled. It was painful to fall, but once he learned it well, it was relatively easy to run.

No one lives flawlessly. If we look closer, everyone has blemishes and cracks. We all are fragile clayware. When we admit our fragility, our healing and recovery begins. If we keep running forward, believing we are so self-sufficient and capable, we will eventually hear the sound of cracks. We get money but relationships break. We attain fame, but our family can break. This is not happiness. The wise will check any broken area of life and ask for God's healing before continuing the race.

A young church member was wearing a T-shirt that said, "Life is fragile. Handle with prayers." I thought he realized a very good point of life early on.

Everybody can break. Regardless of age and environment, we all can break. But when we admit our fragility and want to remedy it, we get an opportunity to recover. In contrast, it's hard to give this opportunity to someone who acts as a perfectly capable person to handle anything. How would God take this when even a mere human being can spot many weaknesses and faults? When we humbly accept our weaknesses and ask for his grace, he will give a blessing to make us anew.

A Vessel That Pleases God

Israel was like a broken vessel. God warned them sternly. He told them to blow the trumpet when the enemy came. There were two situations when they blew the trumpet in the ancient days. First, when they won a war or had something to celebrate, they blew the trumpet of joy. Another time was when they were expecting a danger like an invasion of enemies. It was the trumpet of a warning.

God said, "Put the trumpet to your lips! An eagle is over the house of the Lord" (Hos 8:1). "The house of the Lord" generally means a temple or sanctuary, but in this context, we can take its meaning as all of Israel. God warned that an enemy would invade and sweep Israel swiftly as an eagle captures its prey. He told Israel to blow the trumpet.

Why did this happen? It was because Israel broke the covenant and rebelled against God's law. A disaster befell them due to sin. Let us ponder what a covenant means for a moment. If there was one word that covered and summarized all of the Bible, it would be "covenant." The Old Testament is an old covenant, and the New Testament is a new covenant. A controlling purpose of the entire Hosea book is also God's covenant. Here a "controlling purpose" means a core concept that drives and leads main messages of a passage in biblical hermeneutics. God held onto the corrupt and rebellious Israel because of his covenant. It bound Israel to God.

A covenant is a personal promise between two beings. In general, a new relation begins with a covenant. It's not an official relation until making a covenant, no matter how much time they spent together. An example would be an unmarried couple who knew each other for a long time. Until they made a covenant of marriage, they would still be technically strangers. Only a covenant can establish with authority a marital relationship and its responsibility to each other. Once a covenant is established, a married couple should not separate through thick and thin. They vowed to stay together "till death do us part." Americans say they need three rings for a marriage. They are an engagement ring, a wedding ring, and suffering. It means we need long suffering and patience to make a marriage last.

A covenant is a string that connects relationships. So when it gets broken, relationships get broken as well. A covenant also binds love. So when it breaks, love breaks down, too. In a relationship with God, a covenant is a passage of salvation and blessings. So if it breaks, everything breaks.

In the book of Genesis, God created man and made a covenant to have a relationship. God allowed man to live in the garden of Eden, prohibiting eating from only one tree. It was the tree of knowledge of good and evil. Adam and Eve were able to eat from many trees but were forbidden to eat from this particular tree. This was his covenant. We cannot fully grasp why this was needed by God; however, a relationship began. From then on, God protected, loved, and blessed mankind.

Israel had the same kind of relationship with God. God called Abraham then made a covenant with him. Abraham and his descendants, the Hebrews, entered a special relationship with God. There were many other nations. After the Babel tower incident, there came to be many languages and tribes. God chose only one nation among them. It was the Hebrew people that took the name, Israel after Jacob after the exodus. From the moment of making a covenant, Israel became a special being to God. They became a nation that God blessed specially as his own. Israel's people had the privilege of God's presence, words, and blessings that no other nation had access to.

Then someone broke this covenant with God. Was it God? No. Israel's people did. Once the covenant, the bonding of relationships, love, and God's blessings was damaged, Israel came to dislike the good. Goodness is God's characteristic. Israel came to dislike all things related to God. As a result, they appointed king and princes as they pleased. They started living without God. Furthermore, they erected and served idols. This led to the demise of Israel. The book of Hosea described it in a literary fashion: "They sow the wind and reap the whirlwind" (Hos 8:7). All their hard work and effort were only futile and brought on troubles like the whirlwind. "The stalk has no head; it will produce no flour. Were it to yield grain, foreigners would swallow it up" (Hos 8:7). We call this a "minus life." Hard work still leaves us empty with no rewards. We reap no fruits. This was the dire reality of Israel who left God and broke their covenant.

"Israel is swallowed up; now she is among the nations like something no one wants" (Hos 8:8). Their privileged status fell to "something no one wants" after they broke the covenant.

The same goes for our lives. When we accept Jesus as our Lord and Savior, we enter into a covenant relationship with God. It's much like a parent-child relationship. God calls us his children when we accept him, and he grants power and authority. If our relationship with God gets severed, we will become like Israel, a vessel that no one wants.

Let us consider "brokenness" in life. It could be financial, materialistic, physical, or psychological. But the most serious brokenness would be a broken relationship with God. A broken relationship with God leads to the brokenness of the entire life with many repurcussions and much chaos. So it is of vital importance that our broken relationship with God should be mended to become a holy vessel that God is pleased with.

Remember Your First Love

We should remember and recognize the time when we came to love God the first time, if we want to become a holy vessel again. The recovery of our first love is the first step in recovery of our broken vessel. God spoke through prophet Hosea that he would return to Israel again. Israel cries out to me, "Our God, we acknowledge you!" (Hos 8:2).

The present reality was that Israel was damaged like a broken vessel. But in this verse, we find hope in their future. They would "acknowledge" God. After a period of not recognizing the present and living God, they would come to realize his existence and his precious love.

It's typical that we fail to recognize the true worth of something within our reach. Sometimes we just undervalue the things that are easily accessible to us. For example, we fail to recognize the worth of good health while we are healthy. But our perspective changes when we become ill. If we have to undergo a big surgery, then we learn how precious good health is. The same goes for our spouses. We underestimate our wife or husband when they are home every day. But if we were to lose our spouses, it would truly be a big loss. We foolishly acknowledge the value of a close one, only after he or she leaves us.

Similarly, we take God for granted when he is near. We sometimes don't fully realize the value of worship if we can casually come to church and praise. But imagine that we leave God. We will learn the hard way how priceless God's presence is.

It happened to the Northern Israelites. When they lived an abundant life in Israel, they didn't know the true meaning of God's presence. Only after Israel got destroyed and the people were scattered in exile into foreign lands did they finally realize that being able to call on God was such a blessing. Some time after, Southern Judah was in captivity and lived on the riverside in Babylon. They sat by the river and wept, looking unto their homeland. They hung salt on willow trees and had to sing a song that their captors forced them to sing. Had they appreciated God's presence earlier, they wouldn't have been dragged out to Babylon. They realized late.

Though late, if you long for God again, that is a start. It is common that people give up out of despair after they go through failures. When you have failed, trust in God who still loves you. Come before him, and you will be on the road to recovery. We should remember the love we felt when we first met God. Call on God with all your heart and take time to come before his throne. God still loves us, even when we fail. He still waits for us and wants to heal us. He will touch our brokenness, treat it, and renew us. If we want to be a vessel that God uses, we need to recognize our love to him again.

Change Your Spiritual Desire

We should change our spiritual desire in order to be transformed into a holy vessel of God. We should not stop at recognizing God's presence and love. We should update our spiritual desire completely. When we accept Jesus as our Lord and Savior, we get saved. Our status changes. We are moved from death to life. But if we stop here, we cannot grow to become God's good instruments. We need to adjust our spiritual taste as well to be truly transformed.

Israel had already departed from the good, so it was inevitable that they had to face enemies. As a result of leaving God, their spiritual taste or preference changed. They came to dislike goodness. The characteristics of God are goodness and righteousness. Israel was at odds with God's characteristics. This is an unfortunate byproduct of a broken relationship with God. When our hearts are filled with physical or secular things, not serving God as the Lord, we are not at ease with God. If possible, we prefer avoiding him. As apostle Paul said, the desire of the body and the desire of the spirit oppose each other.

Therefore, we have to straighten our spiritual tendency. We have to align our hearts and their fundamental desire with God's characteristics.

Spirit-filled people always feel joy when they think upon God's work. What God pleases is also their joy. They look forward to worshiping and praying. On the other hand, people occupied with physical desires lighten up when it comes to enjoyment and pleasures, while their faces darken at the hour of a worship service. It's due to their different spiritual desires. The latter group express annoyance when they are invited to early-morning prayer, intercessory prayer, or group prayer times. They say they want some space to feel comfortable and live their faith undisturbed. To these people, coming to church on Sundays is already a generous participation on their part.

But when we are filled with Spirit, our spiritual cores change. We long for the worship, prayer, and praise hour, which used to be a nuisance and burden. Especially in the evangelical or missional areas, we may show a big growth. It becomes possible to pray for another soul that we don't even know. This is because we are following the footsteps of Jesus in the Holy Spirit.

What can be more transformative than this in our lives? Let us leave our old ways of pursuing physical desires. Instead let us follow the Spirit with our renewed minds. We will then give off the fragrance of Jesus Christ. Many people will be inspired. Even if we may be broken vessels at present, we can be transformed into new vessels through healing. We can renew our minds in the Holy Spirit.

Go Back to the Origin

We have to go back to our original places in order to be molded into God's holy pot. The original place where we should anchor our roots of faith is God, our potter. Israel in the past abandoned God and made idols out of gold and silver. Covered with gold, an idol is still only a piece of wood. It doesn't embody life. The calf of Samaria, a manmade idol, will surely be destroyed. There is no power in idols that are like products in a factory.

The golden calf idol was the worst and heaviest sin committed by the people of Israel. Jeroboam, the first king of the Northern Kingdom of Israel, erected golden calves at temples of Bethel and Dan. He feared that the people would admire Jerusalem for its holy temple. Out of his own will, he created golden calves and told his people that these were the "gods that saved them out of Egypt." The truth is, the golden calves are breakable. Israel's recovery will be contingent upon their turning away from futile idols and returning to the living God.

The prophet Jeremiah explained with a potter analogy. A potter was making clayware, and some broke into pieces. Generally potters throw away all the broken wares. However, this potter was different. He reused and re-molded the broken clay to make a new pot. God also said to Israel. "Like clay in the hand of the potter, so are you in my hand, Israel" (Jer 18:6).

The place where Israel should be is in God's hands. Our spiritual home should be in God's hands as well. Although we may be marred or broken, in his hands, we can be fixed and re-formed to be new pots.

Everyone is subject to becoming broken. We all have our brokenness in a physical, emotional, mental, or relational area. Who alone can fix our broken lives? We certainly cannot do it ourselves. Only God, our potter, can.

So come to God and confess your broken reality. We don't need to pretend that everything is going well. We don't need to act as if we have no hurts, blemishes, or pain. Come to God as you are. The Holy Spirit will anoint you with oil. He will lay his hands on us, command, and heal our wounds. We will once again be his holy pot, a passage of blessings to many others.

3

A Daystar Rises at Dawn

[1] After Saul returned from pursuing the Philistines, he was told, "David is in the Desert of En Gedi." [2] So Saul took three thousand able young men from all Israel and set out to look for David and his men near the Crags of the Wild Goats.

[3] He came to the sheep pens along the way; a cave was there, and Saul went in to relieve himself. David and his men were far back in the cave. [4] The men said, "This is the day the Lord spoke of when he said to you, 'I will give your enemy into your hands for you to deal with as you wish.'" Then David crept up unnoticed and cut off a corner of Saul's robe.

[5] Afterward, David was conscience-stricken for having cut off a corner of his robe. [6] He said to his men, "The Lord forbid that I should do such a thing to my master, the Lord's anointed, or lay my hand on him; for he is the anointed of the Lord." [7] With these words David sharply rebuked his men and did not allow them to attack Saul. And Saul left the cave and went his way.

—1 SAM 24:1–7

FORGIVING AND LOVING

The silver divorce has become a recent trend in South Korea. We may wonder why these older adults of retirement age would decide on a divorce after having been together so long. I took interest in reading this newspaper article on a divorce case of a couple in their sixties. What was unique about their case was that the wife who filed for a divorce didn't have a particular reason. Her husband neither cheated on her nor failed to provide for family. He was even a fairly wealthy man who made a comfortable living for his family. Their children grew up well and had families of their own. When asked why she wanted a divorce, she said it was because he wounded her deeply in their early marriage days. It seemed that he might have used physical and verbal abuse. She said he was disrespectful and cold to her mother. He mistreated her and her family for being poor. She became resentful and wanted to pay it back. So as soon as their youngest got married, she ended the marriage of forty years.

Would the divorce be sufficient revenge? Would she be completely satisfied? I highly doubt it. It's more likely that her heart ached in emptiness. A life can be full of wounds. If we harbor resentment and anger in our hearts, we give negative influence not only to others but to ourselves the most. Therefore, we need to learn to address our anger and hurts properly, forgive, and make peace. It may not be easy, but I encourage all of us to sweep the lumps in our hearts and forgive others. Let us bless others with glad hearts and love one another.

To Forgive and Love

Saul caused deep hurt to David. He was jealous of David for no justified reason and tried to kill him multiple times. Eventually David was driven into a wilderness and had to endure a time of suffering, wasting his youth. Saul craftily sent troops to close in on David whenever he was exhausted. When David was in the desert of En Gedi, Saul set out to look for him with three thousand men.

Then an unexpected incident occurred. Saul went into a cave as he needed to go to bathroom. By coincidence, David and his men were hiding in that very cave. Entering from outside, Saul probably couldn't see the dark inside very well. But David and his men saw Saul clearly. It would have been a perfect opportunity to strike him when he was unguarded. Understandably David's men tried to persuade him, saying it was a sign of God's help. As this was a perfect moment to execute his revenge for all the pain and suffering Saul caused him over years, they said to go ahead and strike him. But all David did was to cut off a corner of Saul's robe from behind. David even stopped his men from attacking Saul and just let him get away.

Although his enemy was within his reach, he forgave and protected him instead of taking his revenge.

A similar incident happened another time. Saul was lying asleep inside the camp, and the soldiers were all asleep, unguarded. David and Abishai went to the army and saw that Saul's spear was stuck in the ground near his head. It would be the end of Saul if they just picked up the spear and struck him once. But David didn't take revenge. He only took the spear and water jug that were near Saul. David's choice was not an easy one at all. Saul trampled upon David's life, left him deep scars, and made him waste away youth in the wilderness. And the perfect opportunity of revenge was right in front. David still didn't strike him. He didn't just pretend to forgive him. He truly forgave Saul from a place of love, deep in his heart. Later David actually wept and fasted in grief upon hearing of Saul's death by a Philistine.

We can mimic forgiveness. We can pretend to forgive someone. But it's nearly impossible to love wholeheartedly and bless the very person who hurt you badly. How was it possible for David to take such a risk in love?

Meditate on God's Will

What enabled David to forgive Saul was that David thought of God. To be more precise, he revered, honored, and meditated on God's will. "But the Lord forbid that I should lay a hand on the Lord's anointed" (1 Sam 26:11).

He didn't withhold from striking Saul because Saul was not guilty. It wasn't because David didn't harbor anguish towards him either. What mattered more to David was God's perspective on this situation. He was able to look beyond his own emotions and personal resentment. He cared about how God would view his actions. Saul was a king anointed by God after all. If God raised him up, it should also be God who took him down. Taking over God's role and putting our emotions first would be dishonoring God. It would be against God's will. So David did not lay his hands on God's anointed. He faithfully asked God to be the judge to handle it. He surrendered all his baggage and will to take revenge into his own hands over to God.

God warned against taking matters into our own hands and said that it is up to him. Let us be mindful of God's perspective first, rather than our own emotions and desires. Our behavior and attitude will be different. David accepted God's will out of reverence and put his personal agenda aside.

What result did David's God-centered attitude bring about? First Saul was moved. He wept and confessed his sin. He prayed to God to bless David after having chased him to kill him. We learn how God handled Saul's crimes and sin. We also learn how God blessed David, who leaned on God. God poured grace onto David to become the ruler of Israel.

Taking matters into our hands may appear to be a fast track. But let us have faith and surrender them to God. He can do better. The result will be more fabulous in God's hands. Let us not fall into temptation to be the judges. Leave them in God's hands. "In all things God works for the good of those who love him, who have been called according to his purpose." Let us meditate on God's will first.

Look Back on Yourself

We have to look back on ourselves to love and bless those who hurt us. Only those who can look in themselves are able to forgive others. It's in human nature that we see the faults of others well while we are blind to our own. We so easily criticize and attack others. Forgiveness begins when we examine ourselves. The moment we realize our own shortcomings and limitations, forgiveness and healing can begin.

In general, there are four steps in a forgiving process. The first step is when we get hurt. We could get hurt by unthoughtful remarks, various offenses and insults, or betrayals by a trusted person. The second step is the hating period. It doesn't usually end with being hurt. We begin to hate and resent our perpetrators. We are supposed to meditate God's words, but we dwell in hatred instead. What would happen then? Our spirit will dwindle and our hatred will increase. Therefore, harboring hatred and resentment is never wise.

The next step is the healing period. We need a shift in perspective at this stage. We need to change our views and thoughts. We need to get out of our narrow self-centric frame, and re-illuminate the situation with another perspective. We can try to understand the heart and motive of our perpetrators for their actions. Then we can take a further step to reflect on our own shortcomings. A healing will have begun when we make such an attempt to shift our perspective. Healing goes hand in hand with remembering that we were sinners and we were forgiven at the cross by grace. Through this healing process, we will become ready to embrace others and forgive. This last step is the actual forgiving step.

David did not call himself righteous. In many places in Psalms, David confessed how he is full of sin and faults before God. "For troubles without number surround me; my sins have overtaken me, and I cannot see. They are more than the hairs of my head, and my heart fails within me" (Ps 40:12). David realized his many sins whenever he was standing before God's grace. So he couldn't submit his complaints regarding Saul's wrongdoings as he was aware of his own faults. Let us recall what crime David ended up committing on his throne. He coveted another man's wife, Bathsheba, and so sent Uriah to a battlefront to get him killed. David was not different from Saul in that he also was a fallible human being who can commit an unspeakably evil crime. The same goes for us. We cannot be overly trusting of our own righteousness and be quick at judging others for their faults nearsightedly. It's easier to condemn than forgive as humans. In order to forgive and accept others, we need to take a good look at our own shortcomings with humility.

I heard the following testimony of a deacon who was doing a Q.T. (Quiet Time, a daily meditation of the word) ministry in Daejeon, South Korea. She came to see her friend living in Seoul after a long while, and they had fun conversations. But intermittently she heard some thorny remarks during that time. On the way back home, those thorny remarks started to poke at her heart. The more she remembered them, the more she felt annoyed. She felt wronged and very angry at last. So she decided to go back to Seoul and take her revenge. She wanted to pay her back with more powerfully worse comments that would be a bigger blow to her.

The next morning she opened the Bible to do her daily Q.T. The passage of that day was the following from the book of Ecclesiates: "Do not pay attention to every word people say, or you may hear your servant cursing you, for you know in your heart that many times you yourself have cursed others" (Eccl 7:21–22). The passage came to her like a wake-up call. She realized that she only remembered spiteful comments that her friend said, not her own. She realized that she was just like her. Her perspective shifted at that moment. She assumed that she was only a victim, but she could be a perpetrator to someone else. She repented about her last night then prayed to God to bless her friend. She praised God who made her see with a new perspective.

No one is blameless. In front of our mirror called the cross, we are all indebted to forgiveness. The forgiveness we received from God is incomparable to the forgiveness we may give to others. To borrow Jesus' analogy, we are like the man whose huge debt of ten thousand talents was forgiven, yet was extremely harsh towards another who owed him only a hundred denarius. We should not put our debted in jail. We should realize how ungenerous and unforgiving we can be towards others, when we received thousands of undeserving blessings. When we look into ourselves, we can enter the next steps of healing and forgiving.

Receive the Power of the Holy Spirit

We also need to receive the power of the Holy Spirit in our forgiving process. There was a turning point in David's life, which also became his motivation to be able to forgive Saul. David was anointed by the prophet Samuel. At that time God's spirit came upon him. But David still did not ascend to the throne yet, and to make it worse, he was on the brink of dying due to treason. His life was already at a crossroad, although the door of his next ministry was not fully open yet. A new chapter already had begun as God's angel was with him. David's victory over Goliath and the Philistine army was a great feat. But his faithful attitude in the wilderness was an even greater feat. He did not resent God and praised him in his suffering. That was a true power, and it came from the Holy Spirit's anointing. David could spare Saul's life when he could easily take it for revenge. That was possible in the power of the Holy Spirit, not his own will.

Our efforts do not enable us to forgive someone. Do not fret to forgive. There is hardly anything more difficult. Our deep-rooted wounds do not get healed overnight. Just come before the cross of Jesus Christ. Give him our baggage and ask for the power of the Holy Spirit. Let us decide to live in the Holy Spirit.

It was a time of benediction at the end of a praise night. A woman came up to a leading pastor to receive a healing prayer. He tried hard to pray for her and give blessings. But it was not easy. The lady also received the prayer but looked unrelieved. Her heart was filled with something else, so the praying felt difficult. The pastor paused and asked her to share anything that was blocking her heart. So her counseling began.

Her husband was a well-to-do doctor who graduated from a top university in Korea. To satisfy her husband's family, she prepared and gave a huge wedding gift package called "honsu" in Korea. However, a marriage that exchanged materials with desirable conditions such as a good job and income was not happy. Her husband did not love her. He had an affair after affair, and she began to be resentful through her long and lonely nights. She was a church goer. She attended Sunday services and prayed. But God's grace didn't come upon her, as her heart was not right. Showing up at church or sitting though prayer meetings does not guarantee our personal experience to receive God's grace. If our hearts are filled with hatred, God's power cannot work with them. A blockage of our hearts is a serious problem.

After hearing of her story, the pastor advised her to empty out the hatred inside. How would she do this? He advised her to confess the hatred in her heart before the cross and proclaim her forgiving her husband. She initially declined. If there were one person she couldn't forgive, it would be her husband. She kept on resisting, but finally she joined a prayer with the pastor's encouragement. As soon as the prayer began, she burst into tears. The lumps in her heart were poured out. After she emptied her heart out, God began to work in her.

Her life transformed after this. Her face brightened up, and her physical illness was healed some months later. She even joined a church ministry.

When we have lumps of hatred in our hearts, we are unable to receive God's grace. We all need the blood of the lamb on the cross. We all need the power of the Holy Spirit. We cannot will to love someone. Our efforts and doings do not enable us to forgive others. It's only possible in the power of the Holy Spirit.

First, flush out your inner wounds. Confess hatred that you have harbored in your heart for a long time. Ask the Lord for help, so you can forgive others as he forgave us.

GOD WILL FILL US

> There was also a prophet, Anna, the daughter of Penuel, of the tribe of Asher. She was very old; she had lived with her husband seven years after her marriage, and then was a widow until she was eighty-four. She never left the temple but worshiped night and day, fasting and praying. Coming up to them at that very moment, she gave thanks to God and spoke about the child to all who were looking forward to the redemption of Jerusalem. (Luke 2:36–38)

A married couple was going out on a holiday weekend. The husband was waiting at the door, but the wife was not coming out. Generally it doesn't take too long for men to get ready. After a long wait, the husband ran out of patience and shouted at her, asking when she would be ready. The wife responded, annoyed, "I told you an hour ago that it would be just a short while."

Let us not forget that "a short while" can be an hour to women. People have different standards and notions of time. God's time also differs from our time. An act of faith would be acknowledging this difference and waiting on God's time. We often argue with God, "Why don't you respond already? I'm in so much pain. What's your delay about?"

We need to remember one important fact. God is never late. He always keeps his time. It is us being impatient while waiting. Our faith can mature as we wait for his time with patience, when not everything has come together yet or the circumstances are not as desired. Another benefit of waiting until his time in faith is that we see the perfect blessings that he planned at his time. We should wait in faith until God's time.

To Wait until God's Time

There was an exemplary woman who tasted the fruits of joy through her faith of waiting. "There was also a prophet, Anna, the daughter of Penuel, of the tribe of Asher. She was very old; she had lived with her husband seven years after her marriage, and then was a widow until she was eighty-four" (Luke 2:36). She was the prophet Anna. The book of Luke recorded the Anna was from the tribe of Asher. Asher was the eighth out of Jacob's twelve sons and was born of a female handmaid, Zilpah. So it was not a reputable family like Joseph or Judah. Anna also became widowed when her husband died seven years into their marriage. She lived at the sanctuary by herself, and there was no mention of her children. So we can assume that she probably had no family to support her. In short, she had an unfortunate fate and lived under an undesirable circumstance. However, the prophet Anna knew a precious secret. It was "waiting." She had a heart of waiting for the return of the Messiah.

God's people were suffering under Roman oppression. They were overtaken by Assyria, Babylon, and the Roman Empire. They endured a dark period. Anna had a conviction that after the presently dark and disgraceful period, the Messiah would return and abolish all forces of evil and shame. This waiting period persisted until she turned eighty-four years old.

It was long enough of a time for people, governments, and surroundings to change around her. In those years she waited only for the Messiah. We can imagine such a waiting period must have been boring, disappointing, or frustrating. It is not an easy thing to wait for someone that long. But Anna persisted and eventually received the blessing of seeing baby Jesus herself. She had the exclusive privilege of looking at Jesus Christ up closely and witnessing God's fulfilling his promise.

We all have waiting periods in our lives. It's because our lives are yet incomplete. Due to incomplete assignments, our lives cannot be fully recovered. Despair and pain are still there. Our spouses or children may still be gone and not return. Our bodily illnesses may still remain and plague our present reality. God intends these to be left as works-in-progress in our lives. He wants us to be in waiting. We have to wait patiently although the unfinished assignments can be hard and frustrating. God makes us mature as we wait. In his time all the unfinished assignments will be completed. Only those who wait until that time will experience God's blessings perfectly in full scale.

Therefore we have to learn to wait. Let us wait in God. Let us learn to be patient and keep hoping for God's great blessings in the future. Many of us have impatience syndrome. Have you ever pressed the "close" button in an elevator because you couldn't wait another two to three seconds? We have to discipline ourselves to wait and fight our natural tendency to get impatient. Now let us look into the principles of waiting to help us patiently wait until his time.

The Principle of the Covenant

We need to hold onto his covenant if we want to wait till the right time. As Christians, we should not aimlessly wait. We wait to honor the covenant. An aimless waiting makes our lives only pointless. God already assigned a clear objective to wait for and also gave instructions to us on how to wait. If we hold to his promise, not giving up, then we will be able to reap the good fruits of waiting.

Anna was a prophet. Female prophets are few in the Bible. They include Miriam, Moses' sister, Huldah who explained the Law to King Josiah, and Noadiah who interfered with Nehemiah's ministry. Anna was also a female prophet whose main work was waiting at sanctuary.

A prophet's duty is to hear God's message and proclaim it. Prophet Anna had a message that God gave and impressed in her mind. So she didn't just wait without a clear purpose but waited while holding onto the messianic message from God.

God's promise made it possible for her to wait for many years.

Anna probably held onto the following prophecy from the book of Isaiah, too.

> The desert and the parched land will be glad;
>   the wilderness will rejoice and blossom.
> Like the crocus, [2] it will burst into bloom;
>   it will rejoice greatly and shout for joy.
> The glory of Lebanon will be given to it,
>   the splendor of Carmel and Sharon;
> they will see the glory of the Lord,
>   the splendor of our God.
> [3] Strengthen the feeble hands,
>   steady the knees that give way;
> [4] say to those with fearful hearts,
>   "Be strong, do not fear;
> your God will come,
>   he will come with vengeance;
> with divine retribution
>   he will come to save you."
> [5] Then will the eyes of the blind be opened
>   and the ears of the deaf unstopped.
> [6] Then will the lame leap like a deer,
>   and the mute tongue shout for joy.
> Water will gush forth in the wilderness
>   and streams in the desert. (Isa 35:1–6)

The above is probably the most beautiful one among numerous prophecies about the Messiah. This passage describes the blessings which will be revealed upon the Messiah's return. It says, "The desert and the parched land will be glad; the wilderness will rejoice and blossom." It also says, "He will come with vengeance; with divine retribution. He will come to save you." Israel was situated between stronger nations and was invaded multiple times. They longed for the Messiah who would save them. He would "strengthen the feeble hands" and save the people in bondage. He would also cure all illness-stricken people, as the main work of the Messiah is healing. God promised his works in healing, recovery, releasing from bondage, and power.

Anna kept God's promise close to her heart, so she was able to firmly stand and wait in the dark and painful reality. Let us apply it to our lives. What would be a sure guarantor in our lives in this world? Would wealth ensure our happiness and being alive? It would not.

Consider the financial market shock that happened in Dubai in November of 2009. It made big ripples across the world. The stock markets plunged worldwide, and the Korean stock market was also shaken. Dubai was a nation in Arab Emirates and had a high reputation of being a miracle in the desert at the time. It had only 1.3 million people in population but was able to pull in massive investments, leveraging its natural oil resources. Buildings were built in the middle of the desert, and man-made lakes and islands were created. It loudly advertised itself as a paradise. As money made more money, more investments were probably flowing into the nation. But it eventually ran into troubles. The Dubai World Trade Centre declared a moratorium as it couldn't meet the payment obligation. This led to a brief hiccup in the cash flow, which then caused a big shock to the world economy.

Today's prosperity does not guarantee tomorrow's prosperity. What can guarantee happiness at all times?

If you are a golf fan, you would know Tiger Woods well. He was the most successful sports star in this century. He was a legend. So many people admired him like an idol. Then articles about his scandals flooded media. Unfortunately we see fallen celebrities that have lost all their fame, reputation, and success due to personal scandals from time to time.

It is certain that appearance is not everything about a person. It could take only a moment to endanger a family. No one can be so sure of their footing in life.

Therefore, Christians should live, holding onto the words of Christ. We should not be swayed by or follow the world's media or polls. We should not follow the logic of economics or the current trends in politics. We can stand firmly and upright only when we hold onto God's promise. We will not be shaken even when the world shakes us. If we have strong convictions in faith, we can follow God's will on the right path, no matter what others say to us. If we keep waiting in faith, we will get to taste the fruit of the waiting in his time.

The Principle of Staying

Next is the principle of staying, not leaving the place of waiting. To reap and taste the fruits of waiting, we have to stay in our place. And that place is the sanctuary. Prophet Anna never left the temple. She stayed put and waited for the Messiah. Why a sanctuary? It was a place where God was present.

Before a temple was built, a tabernacle acted as a temple. A tabernacle was a place of God when Israelites were living in the wilderness. They had to come up to the tabernacle to worship God. So its nickname was a tent of meeting. Israelites met and communed with God in the tent.

The tent or temple was a main spiritual center where humans could meet God, have a relationship with him, learn his will, and also receive power. So it would not be right to wait just anywhere in the world. We should stay right in God's place for him.

Let us also keep our faith while waiting. Then we will not be shaken until the time God replies. Our hope will not be fulfilled if we wait in any random manner as we please. We should wait in him. In our uniquely assigned spiritual place and in the sanctuary, we should wait. Only if we remain in our assigned positions until his time will God fill us.

Right before Jesus ascended into heaven, he told his disciples to stay in Jerusalem "until you have been clothed with power from on high" (Luke 24:49). They had not yet experienced the Holy Spirit and so didn't understand what "the power from on high" meant. Nonetheless, they followed Jesus' command and stayed in the city.

We may wonder why the power from God must be poured specifically onto Jerusalem. From the disciples' standpoint, Jerusalem was not a place of their preference. Their teacher was persecuted there. It was still dangerous for themselves to stay in, as Roman officials or Jewish religious leaders might arrest them. Although Jesus told them to stay in Jerusalem, a more reasonable choice would have been leaving the city. But still, the disciples obeyed and stayed. After ten days of fervent praying, they got to experience a very special milestone in Christian history as the Holy Spirit came upon them on the day of Pentecost.

Had they left the city, they wouldn't have been part of that fulfillment. The Holy Spirit probably still came, as God's promise was to be fulfilled. However, the disciples would not have witnessed and experienced the coming of the Holy Spirit themselves.

After the resurrection of Jesus, he appeared before five hundred followers simultaneously. From this incident, we can speculate that there were at least 500 disciples of Jesus. Notice there were only 120 when the Holy Spirit came on the day of Pentecost. That leaves us 380 who missed the live moment of God's glory. They had left their posts. When we leave our posts, we cannot receive the power when God comes to pour it on us.

So let us remain in our assigned places and receive his power. There are uniquely assigned places for leaders, ministers, and God's churches, respectively. We must remain and not leave our positions. We have a natural tendency to stop when we run into obstacles or hardships. We try to just give up and leave. But God's grace cannot be delivered to those who stop and leave.

God can pour his power onto us if we keep our posts through challenges. So whatever deters us, let us wait in faith. This is the principle of staying.

The Principle of Looking Above

The last principle in waiting until God's time is the principle of looking above. In other words, it means waiting prayerfully. Prophet Anna fasted day and night and prayed. She did not just pass the time in the sanctuary. She actively prayed. Praying infers that she left a window into heaven wide open and kept looking above and beyond for God's response.

What came about as a result of her continuous prayer and fasting? "Coming up to them at that very moment, she gave thanks to God and spoke about the child to all who were looking forward to the redemption of Jerusalem" (Luke 2:38). "At that very moment," like a coincidence, something happened. She ran into the baby Jesus. There was God's will in all of this. "At that very moment" the parents of Jesus brought the baby to the temple.

Jews performed a purification ceremony to their newborns. It was to purify the body. They did it forty days after birth for male babies and eighty days after birth for female babies. One may think there was a gender discriminating factor in the ceremony, but some interpret differently. As women gave birth to new lives, the female babies were believed to need twice the amount of purification. They typically gave one lamb as an offering, but they gave a pair of doves or pigeons instead if they were poor. Based on the offerings Joseph and Mary gave, we can guess they were quite poor.

Thus when they showed up at the temple to consecrate their baby, the prophet Simeon approached them first and blessed the baby with a prayer. This was the origin of the Child Dedication ceremony that Baptist churches practice today. As the name explains, it dedicates a child to the Lord. While other denominations give baptism for underage children, Baptist churches only acknowledge baptism of adults. So they do the Child Dedication to babies. The parents commit to raising their babies in faith publicly. While Joseph and Mary were doing this child dedication ceremony with prophet Simeon, Anna happened to see baby Jesus. This well-timed coincidence was in fact God's work. He prepared a perfect timing.

Who would God give a blessing of the perfect timing to? He gives to the one who was waiting prayerfully. If you don't hear an immediate answer to your prayer, please do not worry. God already has prepared a perfect timing for it.

God's perfect time certainly exists. Anna stayed at the temple until she was eighty-four years old. She prayed continually with her window open to heaven. God allowed her a privilege of meeting baby Jesus in person in her lifetime. Additionally God poured special grace on her so she could proclaim the coming of baby Jesus to many Jews waiting on the return of the Messiah.

Our lives also need a window to prayer. It is quite difficult to wait as we pray. But all that time we may spend praying and looking above will never be a waste. Consider Daniel who became prosperous in Babylon. As a captive, he prayed three times every day with his window of prayer open towards Jerusalem.

People who pray are not afraid of worsening circumstances. They don't become disheartened by persecutions. It's because their window of prayer to heaven is open. When everything else in life such as our environments and relationships might be closed, the window of prayer to heaven can never be closed. Let us come to God through our prayer and receive his power. Let our lives be blessed and filled by the faithful God.

Some years ago a Jesus Evangelism organization had invited professor Hyun-shik Kim as a guest speaker for a North Korea Mission Seminar they hosted. Professor Kim taught Russian for thirty-eight years at the Pyung-yang College of Education, then escaped North Korea via Russia into South Korea, then the United States. He received the gospel in the United States and became a baptized Christian. He was probably the first of very few North Koreans who converted to Christianity.

He gave the following testimony of how he came to faith. His mother was a devout Christian. She had passed away in North Korea when he was only fifteen. On her death bed, she wished that her son become a follower of Jesus Christ. He couldn't immediately obey her last will. To become successful, he joined the Communist Party and was an activist of atheism. He thought that it would be absurd if an intellectual like himself, who taught at the College of Education, was fooled by an illogical and unrealistic religion.

After some time, he went to Russia as an exchange professor in 1992. His older sister came to see him after forty-two long years. She had moved to Chicago during the Korean War. She was a devout Christian at the time and flew all the way to Russia just to see her younger brother and take him to the United States where she lived. As soon as she saw him, she mentioned their mother's death wish and testified about Jesus Christ.

Would it be easy for someone who was immersed in communist philosophy for forty years to receive the gospel? His heart was unmoved and nothing could persuade him.

It was time for her to depart and she showed her knees. "Brother, our mother's dying wish was for you to believe in Jesus Christ. For that wish, I have prayed every single day for the last forty years." Would you imagine the knees that kneeled for forty years? Professor Kim started opening his heart after seeing the evidence of forty years of prayer. He eventually left North Korea and accepted Christ as his Lord and Savior. He became a faithful servant.

Before the praying knees, all strongholds fall. There is certainly an answer to those who wait for his time and keep on praying. Stubborn hearts and iron walls will surrender. God's power is revealed to those who pray. His amazing works will happen.

We need a waiting period. Let us not be mistaken and just wait being idle. We have to hold onto God's promise. We have to wait in the temple, keeping his will close to our hearts. Most of all, let us pray incessantly and stay on our knees until God answers us. God will surely fill up our holes and make our lives abundant. Our lives are work in progress. There are uncompleted assignments. Let us stay in faith and come to God. In his perfect time, we will reap fruits of joy.

POWER TO UNTANGLE KNOTS

[1] Therefore, my brothers and sisters, you whom I love and long for, my joy and crown, stand firm in the Lord in this way, dear friends! [2] I plead with Euodia and I plead with Syntyche to be of the same mind in the Lord. [3] Yes, and I ask you, my true companion, help these women since they have contended at my side in the cause of the gospel, along with Clement and the rest of my co-workers,

whose names are in the book of life. [4] Rejoice in the Lord always. I will say it again: Rejoice! [5] Let your gentleness be evident to all. The Lord is near. [6] Do not be anxious about anything, but in every situation, by prayer and petition, with thanksgiving, present your requests to God. [7] And the peace of God, which transcends all understanding, will guard your hearts and your minds in Christ Jesus. (Phil 4:1–7)

In April of 2015, KKLA News (LA FM) broadcast very shocking news that alarmed the world. A prisoner who served seventeen years in jail for a murder charge was discovered to be not guilty. Susan Mellen had been sentenced to a lifetime in prison without bail for allegedly killing a homeless person in 1997. That sentence, however, was based on a single witness who turned out to be a habitual liar and member of a crime organization. After the above was uncovered, Susan was released as an innocent person. It was not the first case of an innocent person being put in prison due to lack of evidence. Obie Anthony was another person proven innocent after serving eighteen years in prison.

There is a saying: "Life is like a skein of thread." Everyone initially starts their life on a clean slate like a neat knitting, then life gets messy over time. It gets complex knots of tangled relationships, problems, and situations. Sometimes faults and mistakes of others impact us in a negative way. How can we deal with these unwanted knots in life?

There seem to be three main ways of dealing with those. The first is to leave them as they are. This would cause more entanglements and complications with time, as they are not properly addressed.

The second method is to simply cut off the knots. It would be an easy elimination of the knots, but they won't be usable any more. This method became famous by Alexander the Great. An oxcart was secured with an intricate knot, and an ancient king of Phrygia said that he who could unravel it would become master of Asia. Many young men tried but failed to unravel the complex knot. Alexander sliced the knot in half with his sword. It was such an easy and simple solution. Since then, people called a complex problem that can be solved easily a "Gordian Knot." Actually dictators preferred this method in history. When things got hairy, they sliced the problem with a sword. It may look like a solution that cleans up mess, but it pays no attention to the hurts and pain of the affected people in the process.

The third one is to take time and untangle the knots one thread at a time. Keeping each thread intact and protected is of higher importance than just unraveling the knot. This is also God's way.

When mankind fell into sin, their lives became stained and twisted. Because Adam and Eve didn't obey God and crossed the line, their relationship with God got broken and their lives fell into chaos. God could have used the slicing-off method like Alexander the Great. Sinners probably deserved it. However, God did not react like that. He patiently waited and poured his love and care. When they still did not return, he himself came to earth as man and became the redeeming sacrifice. As children of such a God, we would have to choose a different way from this world. We should not cut knots off like the world does so easily. Let us model after God who demonstrated patience and love by untangling a knot thread by thread. Our lives will be full and beautiful with holy fruits.

How We Tackle Problems in Life

Apostle Paul called the church members in Philippi in the following endearing way: "my brothers and sisters, you whom I love and long for, my joy and crown" (Phil 4:1). We can easily guess how he cherished and loved them. The Philippian church had many strengths to brag about. They were good helpers of Paul and served people with love. They also played a vital role in spreading the gospel with Paul. But even to this role model kind of church, there were problems. They were not a perfect church, as no church is on the earth. To borrow pastor Young-gi Choi's book title, churches are more like hospitals. Sick people go to the hospital. Hospitals are full of sick patients. So how can we expect perfect things there? Like hospitals, people groan and scream in pain at church. The Philippian church was one of them, too.

Apostle Paul suggested a solution as follows. "I plead with Euodia and I plead with Syntyche to be of the same mind in the Lord" (Phil 4:2). Why did he make such a plea? Because they were not of the same mind. If they were, he wouldn't have to make such a plea. They were divided in conflicts.

More details about Euodia and Syntyche are not provided in the text, but we can make a reasonable guess that they might be women. Their names end with an "a" and in Greek, this suggests female. Women's social status was not very high in ancient society. Their roles were not of great significance. But it was different in Phillipi. Women actively participated and held important positions at church. Phillipi was located in Macedonia, which was more liberal than other regions. Let us take note that Lydia, a woman, played a pivotal role when apostle Paul planted a new church in Philippi. She was a business woman who sold purple fabrics (Acts 16). The early ministries of the Philippian church were hosted at Lydia's house. We can conjecture her wealth and leadership based from that. We can also infer that female influence was quite strong at the Philippian church. So the conflict between the two could have been a conflict between two main female leaders at church. The text does not specify the reasons for their conflict among numerous possible reasons.

Let us recap. So the Philippian church started with a female leader's influence, and two leaders were at odds for some reason. The entire church was probably in trouble, like an entangled yarn. What happens when church has internal conflicts? Worship services feel awkward and fellowships become uncomfortable. Members of church divide and form factions. Would prayers be the same? Who would they pray for? If left unaddressed, the church community will suffer. Such a community cannot carry out God-given missions well. It will dishonor God's glory. So apostle Paul mentioned this problem in his epistle. He saw the dire need to resolve their situation to restore the church. His solution can be used not only for the Philippian church members but also for our own individual lives. Let us look at some principles that help us unravel hairy problems in life.

Enter into Christ

First, we need to enter into Christ. The crucial clue to crack a difficult life case is always found in Christ. Apostle Paul used the expression "in the Lord" often in his epistle. "Stand firm in the Lord in this way, dear friends!" Here the commanding verb, "stand firm," is in Greek, "steko," which originated in a military language. It describes soldiers standing firmly without retreating, to face the oncoming enemy soldiers toward them. So the expression "stand firm" implies that the Philippian church was facing external pressures or persecutions. Even if the outside persecution or attack may be intimidating, it means we can win against our enemies if we remain in the Lord.

Another problem in the Philippian church was broken relationships. They existed amongst church leaders as well. The solution for them is to be of the same mind "in the Lord." Being "in the Lord" would be key for unity. A person connecting another person could introduce more problems. When we enter into the Lord, having the same mind is possible.

Paul also pleads, "Rejoice in the Lord always." The origin of true joy is Christ. It's not the world or our possessions. Having a lot of wealth and living comfortably do not give us joy. Being in the Lord does. In short, the key to all problems in life is "in the Lord," whether they are external or internal, relating to the Spirit or the environment.

We cannot attain life until we enter into the Lord. Attending church is not sufficient. Reading the Bible, participating in many ministries, or serving at church does not automatically grant us life. Only when we are truly in the Lord, we receive life. In the Lord we learn love, as true love is the love of Jesus Christ who died on the cross for us. We cannot live abundantly unless we are in the Lord. True power and glory are in the Lord.

Then how can we enter into the Lord? The answer is quite simple. We accept Jesus Christ as our Lord and Savior. He is always near us. "Here I am! I stand at the door and knock. If anyone hears my voice and opens the door, I will come in and eat with that person, and they with me" (Rev 3:20). Jesus is standing right outside the door to our hearts. If we open it and welcome him, he will come in and be with us.

The moment we accept Jesus as our Lord and Savior is the moment we enter into the Lord. Jesus will govern our lives. That will be a sign of living a life in him. We hand over the control to him. The Sovereign Lord will reveal his power and authority in our lives.

I once visited a church member who was battling a serious illness. He was active only a few months prior to my visit. He went to the hospital to get some symptoms checked. They said it was the last stage of lung cancer. More detailed tests revealed that cancerous cells had already spread everywhere. All he could do was to take painkillers to withstand the pain. But even with those, he passed out due to unbearable pain sometimes. When I saw him in person, he looked like an entirely different person. He became very thin and his face was pale. I introduced Jesus to him, and we prayed the acceptance prayer together that day.

Why would we introduce Jesus to someone sick with a grave illness? Shouldn't we talk about their illness? Because Jesus is our true life. We need Jesus in us, as he is the source of life. Without him, there will be no miracle of life. While we take medicine and receive treatments, we still have to accept Jesus, the source of life. When he is in us, his living power can cast out physical illnesses or unclean spirits or break us free from all the chains and cursed bondage. Healing is not possible without Jesus. For this reason, when I meet sick people, I introduce Jesus and pray an acceptance prayer for them. Even when we may lose physical bodies to an illness, we can help save the souls that will go to heaven. Nothing would be more worthy than this.

To live an abundant life, we need to enter into the Lord. Jesus is the true vine, and we are the branches. How can the branches survive if they are not attached to the tree? "I am the vine; you are the branches. If you remain in me and I in you, you will bear much fruit; apart from me you can do nothing" (John 15:5). Apart from the origin of life, Jesus, we cannot live. We cannot receive strength to withstand this world. Therefore, we have to enter and remain in the Lord. In the Lord, we can tackle challenging problems and bear much fruit.

Have a Gentle Heart

Next we will need a generous heart in order to tackle intertwined problems in life. Especially regarding interpersonal relationships, we need a gentle heart. Apostle Paul said to the Philippian church, "Let your gentleness be evident to all. The Lord is near" (Phil 4:5). He used the word "gentleness." "Epiakeia" in Greek could be translated into a variety of meanings. Calvin interpreted it as "perseverance." For example, a heart that does not immediately react but endures a thorny and hurtful comment would be gentle. Alternatively, William Barclay interpreted it as "better than justice." A justice means repaying the way it was received, often in the equal weight or quantity. But what would happen if we were to pay back exactly as we felt hurt in interpersonal relationships? Would it solve problems and restore peace? It would never. So we need something better than serving justice. God also used this method to save us through Jesus Christ.

We all have sinned. And the wage of sin is death. We all deserve judgment which then will send us to hell. This would be serving justice. Since no one is without sin, and sin doesn't just disappear, our God of justice must carry out his justice. No one can face his justice. Ultimately we all have to be sentenced to hell.

However, God sent Jesus Christ as atonement to our sin. We all received grace to salvation. This is "better than justice." The gentleness is better than exact judgment and razor-sharp accusations. We all need this attitude of gentleness in our interpersonal relationships.

It has already been about twenty years since Reverend Dong-myung Kim's wife, Esther Yi-sook Ahn, passed away. I still remember her sermon on Matt 26. I recall that she gave the message either on a Wednesday night or a Sunday afternoon. It was a passage about Jesus praying at Gethsemane.

It was a critical point in time. After that night Jesus was going to be arrested, dragged to the court, put to shame, and nailed to the cross. The night before, Jesus didn't sleep and prayed all night. His heart was desperate as he prepared for the crucifixion. It's written that his sweat was like blood in the Bible.

On the other hand a few disciples slept. Perhaps they even snored. They were Peter, James, and John, the supposedly more faithful ones among them. How disappointed Jesus must have felt. They probably looked unreliable. Yet Jesus said to them, "The spirit is willing, but the flesh is weak" (Matt 26:41).

According to Esther Yi-sook Ahn, this meant "it could happen." Jesus told them, "On a night like this, you all must have been so exhausted that you fell asleep. It could happen." She added that this phrase works magic when it comes to relationship problems. Let us apply this magic when our children are rebellious and offend our feelings. Before we react emotionally to them, please reconsider. Maybe they had a lot of stress from socializing with peers and getting through school. "How tough things must be for them to behave like this. It could happen." We could look at them with a different perspective. A wife may be annoyed at her husband. Wouldn't she be triggered to start an argument, if he acted like a couch potato as soon as he got home and ordered to bring things to him? The wife could think, "He must have had a long day at work. He probably dealt with tough situations and lots of stress. It could happen."

Let me share a story of Mi-kyung Kim. She was a celebrity instructor. She became so popular that people called it a craze for a while, until a scandal of plagiarism broke out. She used to quote her mother's story during her sessions. Her mother was a devout deacon at church, and she prayed early morning every day. Her father was incapable and could not provide for family. He failed at every attempt and lost all the family money. Sometimes neighbors told her mother to just get a divorce. She responded to such comments with wit. "My husband not making money for family is not a reason for a divorce. It is a reason for me to make money. It's quite simple. Why do people get confused?"

When we run into problems, would blaming others take care of them? Blaming another for being incompetent and slow-witted would not do anyone good. Blame is not the solution. We should come before God and follow how he dealt with problems. "It could happen." This is a secret to accept and tolerate one another in hard situations. We can live in blessings with this secret. We have so many intertwined problems that we ourselves cannot unravel. Let us enter into the Lord and embrace others with a gentle heart. Lastly we still need one more.

Believe in the Power of Prayer

The last thing we need to unravel knots in our lives is the power of prayer. God will solve all the unsolved problems if we bring them to him in prayer. Paul said to not be anxious about anything. He said, "in every situation, by prayer and petition, with thanksgiving, present your requests to God" (Phil 4:6). As written in the next verse, the peace of God will guard our hearts and minds.

Worrying is useless. It does not lessen our problems. Often it makes them worse. So Paul said that we should not be anxious and instead pray about everything. When we pray, God takes care of them. When we pray, God is on our side. He intervenes and handles our matters. Prayer hands over our control to God so he can work. He should be in control, not us. His power should execute, not ours. Therefore, praying alone fills our hearts with peace from God.

Prayer is also a privilege, not a duty. Take Korean churches for example. As they had many experiences of the Holy Spirit at work, they held lots of special prayer gatherings. So pastors often encourage church members to show to those prayer meetings. Some members mistake the sincere invitation as a plea, so they take the position of showing themselves to do a favor. But this is a mistake. Prayer is a privilege. If unused, it's a loss to the person who missed the praying opportunity. I encourage us all to use this privilege well.

The Bible also tells us what a great privilege a prayer is. "Let us then approach God's throne of grace with confidence, so that we may receive mercy and find grace to help us in our time of need" (Heb 4:16). Where is the throne of grace? It's in the innermost part of the sanctuary called the most holy place. The lid of the ark of the covenant is called the mercy seat. It's also the throne of grace, where God is present.

The layouts of the sanctuary are slightly different between the Old Testaments and New Testament periods. In the temple built by King Herod, the gentile's courtyard is on the outermost part. The gentiles were allowed only up to that courtyard. Over the wall was the women's garden. The Jewish women could enter there. Next was Israel's garden, which Jewish men could enter. Further inside after that was the priest's courtyard. In this courtyard, priests offered animal sacrifices and gave ceremonies. More inside after that was the sanctuary.

The golden candles, the bread of the presence, and the gold altar of incense were displayed in this sanctuary area. Only the priests could enter, following their prearranged order. If you passed beyond the curtain at the entrance to the tabernacle, there was the most holy place (or holy of holies). As this was the most holy place; only the high priest could access it once a year on the Day of Atonement. Here were the ark of the covenant law and the throne of grace (the mercy seat) on top of it.

Since we are all gentiles, by their rule, we cannot enter even Israel's garden. Because the high priest, Jesus Christ, opened the way for us, we now can pass through Israel's garden, sanctuary, the curtain, and the most holy place. We can come to the throne of grace. This is the highest privilege allowed to Christians. When we pray before the throne of grace, we receive two main benefits. We receive God's mercy and his timely help throughout our lives.

Consider how heavy and burdensome our sins are. Sometimes we cannot sleep, wrestling with guilt before God. Sometimes we are distressed by broken relationships with people. However, if we just come before the throne of grace, we can receive God's mercy, the washing of our sins. As a result, our spirits are cleansed. This is an incredible blessing.

Additionally, we receive the gift of his help whenever we are in need. His help is such that it is precisely what we need at a perfect time when it is needed.

God invites us to his mercy seat. Everything we need is already prepared there. Living water for our thirsty souls is found there. A solution to crack an impossible case is waiting there. All the complex and intertwined knots in our lives can be unraveled at the throne of grace. Therefore I encourage all of us to come before his throne of grace. Come before him and he will start working in your lives.

COMPLETING A MARATHON

> And the God of all grace, who called you to his eternal glory in Christ, after you have suffered a little while, will himself restore you and make you strong, firm and steadfast. To him be the power for ever and ever. Amen.
>
> With the help of Silas, whom I regard as a faithful brother, I have written to you briefly, encouraging you and testifying that this is the true grace of God. Stand fast in it.
>
> She who is in Babylon, chosen together with you, sends you her greetings, and so does my son Mark. Greet one another with a kiss of love.
>
> Peace to all of you who are in Christ. (1 Pet 5:10–14)

Life is a marathon. It's not a short-distance race but is a really long journey. A strong start is good, but finishing the race well is more important. Sometimes we hear of people who give up their life race midway and do not reap the glory of a good finish. Professor Emeritus William Hendriksen, who taught at the Southwestern Baptist School of Theology, pointed out that about two-thirds of the people in the Bible did not finish well. Their starts might have been strong, but for some reason, more than half deviated somewhere along the way.

Why would an end be bad? One reason is that our lives always come with obstacles. This race is not on a flat, straight road. There are many environmental, internal, or spiritual obstacles and distractions. Whatever obstacle befalls us, we need to jump over it and fulfill God's calling for us. We can then be main players that please God in his big picture.

The New York City Marathon is a famous race where over twenty thousand participants including world-class runners gather annually. Generally the winner of the race gets all the spotlight from media. However, according to the New York Times in 2009, the most talked about participant in the year of 1986 ranked only 19,413[th]. That means he was almost the last to finish the race. It was Bob Wieland who completed the marathon over many days. Usually a winner of a marathon completes running the 42,195 km distance in about two hours.

It took much longer time for Wieland because he didn't have 2 legs. He lost both legs at the Vietnam war due to bombing. The lower end of his body trunk was wrapped with protective leather covering, and his fists with special protective covering. He used his hands and arms to push forward at an 1 mile per hour speed.

President Reagan met him in person and asked. "What made you attempt at this tough race?" Bob replied, "Sir, it's too soon to quit." He didn't let disability stop him or give up on living. At his reply, President Reagan called him "Mr. Inspiration."

We need such a mindset. We are prone to quitting at the first sign of obstacles. I see some young people give up quickly on school or full-time jobs when things don't go the way they want. But it's too soon. At some signs of trouble at home, they call it quits. At the unwelcome news of a diagnosis, they just give up on life. God gave each of us only one life to live. If we give up on such a precious gift because of obstacles, then how can we honor God? We are converted Christians. Even those who don't know Jesus keep the will to live and finish their race. As Christians, we should complete our race all the more and fulfill God's calling.

Completing the Race Called Life

The first letter that Peter wrote was received by scattered wayfarers in the Southern part of Asia Minor (roughly today's Turkey peninsula region surrounded by Black Sea, Aegean Sea, and Mediterranean Sea). Here the "scattered wayfarers" refer to the diaspora Jews. To extend this meaning further, they include all Christians that left their homelands and were scattered on foreign lands. We can imagine how exhausting their lives must have been. They didn't have stability to begin with. They lived in a foreign environment where they didn't speak the language. In today's version, they lived an immigrant life. These diaspora Jews faced an additional hardship because the Roman Emperor persecuted Christians. The persecution started first within the boundaries of the Roman Empire, then reached to the outskirts. The recipients of Peter's letter were heavily burdened with persecution on a foreign soil. It would not be easy to keep faith and follow Jesus all the way under such a circumstance. So Peter encouraged them to finish the race even when things were tough. That would be God's will and the essence of a Christian living.

Then how can we stay on course and finish the race? Peter suggested a solution by introducing God as follows. "The God of all grace, who called you to his eternal glory in Christ, after you have suffered a little while, will himself restore you and make you strong, firm and steadfast" (1 Pet 5:10). He described God as "the God of all grace." Take note that the Bible described God in a variety of ways. Some associated authority, justice, or other characteristics with God. Peter called him the God of all grace. God of all grace is the alpha of our lives and the omega of our faith. He knows all about what is happening in our present lives and can offer a perfect solution. He is the almighty God who can help us get back up and rescue us. He alone is the source of power and strength for the wayfarers.

We are unable to finish the race with our own strength. Our efforts and will are not sufficient to overcome all obstacles and live victoriously. Without God's grace it's impossible to complete our race. Peter knew this very well and advised. "This is the true grace of God. Stand fast in it" (1 Pet 5:12).

Generally a letter ended with a closing called doxology, meaning a praise to God. In case of the book of First Peter, it is, "Peace to all of you who are in Christ." After the main part closed, the book added three more verses at the end because Silvanus wrote it in place of Peter. In the ancient days, it was a common practice that another person wrote a letter, as the actual sender spoke the message for multiple reasons. The sender might be of old age or need a translator who can write in Greek. The book of Romans by apostle Paul also had an intermediary, Tertius. Silvanus is assumed to be the same person as Silas, who was Paul's travel companion. Silvanus and Silas are equivalent names in the Roman and Greek styles, respectively. Saul, a Jew, also changed his name to Paul in the Roman form.

To revisit those last three verses at the end, they are treated separately from the main message and are like a signature that shows approval of Paul. Also, it expresses Paul's genuine heart for them. Paul's last closing word for the wayfarers (the diaspora Jews) on foreign soil was "Stand fast in it (God's true grace)."

We can finish our race and complete our missions if we stand strong on solid rocks of God's grace with knowledge of who he is. Life cannot stand by itself. It can be sustained only by God's grace. Without God's help, we cannot run. No one can be successful in life without God's grace, no matter how smart or capable we are. Therefore, it is of vital importance that we seek God's grace in this journey of life full of obstacles.

Are we struggling to stand on our own? Has any of you been injured and broken after such fierce and futile struggles? Let us receive God's grace. God is the "God of all grace." Let us know, hold onto, and run alongside him. We will rise above all obstacles and complete our race to the end. Next let us look further into God's grace.

The Grace of his Touch

The first kind of grace we need from God to complete our marathon is the grace of his touch. His touch means healing. "The God of all grace, who called you to his eternal glory in Christ, after you have suffered a little while, will himself restore you and make you strong, firm and steadfast" (1 Pet 5:10).

God called us. He called us to his eternal glory. This means the gift of salvation to us. While we were sinners, he called us. He made the gospel of his cross known to us and invited us to accept him as the Lord and Savior. We no longer needed to be afraid of the final judgment because we now belonged to heaven. This is the salvation milestone on our journey of faith timeline. From the moment of his calling and salvation to the time we enter heaven, we are in pilgrimage. One inevitable reality on this journey is suffering.

Peter said, "after you have suffered a little while." It wasn't because he took the suffering lightly. No suffering is light and easy. It always entails pain. However, he used "a little while" in comparison to the eternal glory that was awaiting.

Christians are not exempt from suffering. Crises don't just escape them, and big waves don't just die down before believers. Failures happen, too. Even with faith, all sorts of suffering find them. On some level Christians may suffer more due to faith. But there is one crucial difference. Unlike with others, God comes to help and stays alongside Christians in suffering.

When Christians are in suffering for "a little while," God does four things. First, God makes them whole. A Greek word, "katartivzw," means to repair or make whole broken pieces. So in some English translations, they use "mending." It can be used when we realign misplaced joints and put them into proper places. The same word was used when the disciples of Jesus were fixing the broken net. God mends our broken lives. He is the healer. Second, God helps us to stand firm. He builds us up. Third, he gives us strength and energy. Fourth, God makes our foundation firm. As a result, our lives can stand on a firm foundation.

God intervenes and touches our lives to mend and heal. If you have a physical illness, come before God and ask for his touch. His touch will bring healing and recovery. If your spirit is in distress and pain, ask God to touch your spirit. When you face a crisis in family, come before God and ask for his touch. Recovery will begin. Daniel saw a vision about oncoming suffering to Jews. He was so shocked to see such a horrible vision that he collapsed to the ground. When he was fallen on the ground with no strength to get up, there was a hand that touched Daniel. "A hand touched me and set me trembling on my hands and knees" (Dan 10:10).

Who touched Daniel? It was God. He came and touched him to give strength. He said, "Daniel, you who are highly esteemed, consider carefully the words I am about to speak to you, and stand up, for I have now been sent to you" (Dan 10:11). Daniel was completely exhausted after twenty-one days of fasting and seeing the vision. But after hearing this, he was able to get up again and return to his mission. We can take this lesson and apply to our own lives. No matter what problem we face, let us not give up. It's too soon to quit. Let us come before God and ask for his healing. Let us call unto him and seek his grace. With his touch, recovery will begin.

The Grace of Power

The second type of grace we need to complete our race is the grace of power. This power enables us to stand up after recovery. "Peace to all of you who are in Christ" (1 Pet 5:11). In the English versions (NIV, NASB, NKJV), the word "peace" was used. In another version (Korean) "power" was used to translate the Greek meaning of κράτος ("kratos," power, strength). The closing word acknowledged God for being the source of all power. It proclaimed his glory. Although the human ability is limited, God's power is limitless. Nothing is impossible to him. He can make something out of nothing and bless it to be abundant as well. If we can access such power, what problem would be impossible to us? His power is truly limitless. He is the almighty and the creator of all creations. He still operates the entire universe today in his power.

Then how can we tap into his power in our lives? We know of his power but often fail to plug into it from our everyday lives. If we are not connected to the limitless power, then it will be completely useless.

We need two things that help connect us to his mighty power. First is faith and the second is prayer. Faith is the passage of his power, so it can flow to ourselves. Prayer is the passage to our daily lives. His power can be turned on and become active through prayer. When we combine these two, praying in faith, his power can be an active agent in our own experience. We have to pray with such an awareness that our prayer in faith can become actualized in reality, powered by God. So our prayer should not be just a laundry list of our complaints or wants. Our prayer can bring miracles to life.

All the miracles in the Bible were God's works. Israelites could cross the Red Sea and escape the Egyptian military army because God worked a miracle. No strategy or tricks could bring about such a miracle. It was the result of Moses' prayer. He prayed and lifted up a rod, then God's supernatural power came upon Israel. The Red Sea opened. How was it possible for Israelites to fight off the Canaanite tribes and conquer the promised land? It was not the strength of the Israelite army. It was God who destroyed the walls of Jericho and helped Israel become the victor on Canaanite land. Likewise we should pray in faith about everything. We will be connected to God's power which will work miracles in our own lives.

The Grace of Collaboration

We also need the grace of collaboration with our helpers and cheerleaders while we run to complete our race. We cannot run alone. We will be very lonely and less resilient when we fall down. God blesses us Christians with helpers. It is truly God's grace.

God's people were scattered in the southern part of Asia Minor in Peter's time. The diaspora Jews (the biblical dispersion of Israelites or Jews out of their ancient ancestral homeland) might have thought that they were abandoned like orphans on a foreign soil. So Peter reminded them that they had helpers and cheerleaders. "She (church) who is in Babylon, chosen together with you, sends you her greetings, and so does my son Mark" (1 Pet 5:13).

"Church in Babylon" probably meant a church in Rome. Rome in the New Testament period was an equivalent position of Babylon in the Old Testament period. It was a powerful empire in that region. It's possible that he used symbolic language to avoid using the word "Rome" explicitly.

Similarly, the "Babylon" in the book of Revelation also implied Rome. Since Peter mentioned a Roman church, perhaps he was based in Rome when he wrote this letter. Then he wrote this to encourage the Diaspora Jews. He said all the scattered Christians were part of one body in Christ. To those who felt they were alone and isolated, Peter reminded them of a bigger body where they belonged, to cheer on and support them.

Peter also included Mark, calling him "my son." It meant a child in faith. As Timothy was a son of Paul, Mark was like a son and fellow servant in faith to Peter. The reason why Mark could write the book of Mark was because he received the gospel from Peter.

No one can do it all. We all need collaborators. After God created the world, everything looked good in his eyes, except that man was alone. So he created his helper, Eve. He meant humans to live together in a community. Accordingly we should have fellowships with other believers while serving God. Another name for this community is church. We should be grateful for our friends, spouses, and fellow servants in faith, as we journey through our lives.

In church ministries, too, the grace of collaboration is great. Church is not always good and comfortable. Problems and crises come to church. Especially during hard times, it's such a blessing to have people who support and help you. I still keep close to my heart the love and help I received from my collaborators. I wonder if my pastoral ministry would have been even possible without them. Collaborators are truly God-sent and we should be grateful for them. For me, I received grace from the year 1981. I got married that year. I literally cannot live without Grace, as it's my wife's name. Ever since for all those following years, my life simply cannot be defined without grace as well as Grace. Everything came from God.

Sometimes we may mistakenly credit ourselves for all the wins and achievements. If we look closer, we all had someone who helped. Let us not take lightly the value of our collaborators. They are precious. We all need our helpers and cheerleaders to complete our race. When we face hardships, we don't get despaired and can keep running because they are by our side. A life journey is not easy at all. There are all kinds of interferences, distractions, and traps. Let us not give up before any obstacles. It's too soon to quit. Let us remember our God, God of all grace.

When we come before the God of grace, he touches us. He makes us whole and gets us back up. When we are too exhausted or beat to go on, let us pray in faith. He will give us strength. No matter where you are and what the circumstance is, never give up. There are many more miles to run. Do not think about giving up because you feel old. There's no such an age when it's okay to give up. Do not think about giving up because you don't have much wealth or motivation. If God is with you, you can be used for his glory, regardless. We only live once. Like apostle Paul, let us run the race with faith, fight the good fight, and finally stand before God in his glory.

4

In the Morning Silence, Light Shines

[1] Paul, an apostle—sent not from men nor by a man, but by Jesus Christ and God the Father, who raised him from the dead—[2] and all the brothers and sisters with me,

To the churches in Galatia:

[3] Grace and peace to you from God our Father and the Lord Jesus Christ, [4] who gave himself for our sins to rescue us from the present evil age, according to the will of our God and Father, [5] to whom be glory for ever and ever. Amen.

—GAL 1:1–5

PAST NIGHT TO MORNING

The word "conflict" in Korean has its roots in a Chinese word combination of the kudzu tree and wisteria (rattan). They both belong in the category of vine plants. More technically they are in the legume group, but because of their thick stems, we call them trees. So they both tend to wrap around other trees as they are vines, and their flowers are pretty and fragrant. But when they meet, there is usually trouble, because they will intertwine each other, forcing them in the opposite direction. While a kudzu tree tends to spiral to the left, a wisteria tree tends to spiral to the right. So when they run into each other, they will intertwine and pressure each other to cause pain. We call this a conflict.

Because a conflict happens within a near distance, it causes pain in relationships as people feud, bicker, and get divided. It usually does not happen between people who are not in a close relation or contact. Because of nearness and affection, a conflict occurs. It's not uncommon that we see conflicts within married couples or between parents and children or among colleagues at work. We may have conflicts within church communities, too.

A Secret to Overcome Conflicts

Apostle Paul sent epistles to multiple churches that were coping with conflicts. One main example was the book of Galatians. According to the Acts, Paul planted a church in Galatia on his very first missionary journey. In the southern part of Asia Minor, he started many churches in a Roman province, Galatia. He visited each of them on his second and third missionary journeys. We can guess that he thought dearly of them. Then they had conflicts among these churches, too. They were in dispute over Paul's teachings.

Paul had witnessed Jesus Christ and his gospel there. He delivered a message of salvation through faith. After Paul left, Jewish people attacked the churches. These people were the Jews within the church. They emphasized Judaism and importance of the laws. They were against the notion of salvation by faith only. Instead they argued that salvation required circumcision and following the laws of the Jews. To be a Christian, one needed to become a Jew first. This school of thought caused a division. One side followed Paul's teaching while the other side opposed it. One side stood with the gentile church, the Antioch church, while the other side defended the Jerusalem church. They divided, bickered, attacked, and opposed each other.

The door to evangelism and outreach was closed at the churches with internal conflicts. They could not give glory to God. Paul saw this wrenching situation and wrote the book of Galatians to proclaim true freedom of the gospel. Fittingly the theme of this book was "liberating gospel." The gospel freed people from all sins, all laws, and all binding chains. One keyword from this book would be "freedom." So a Bible interpreter even called the book of Galatians the "Magna Carta of Freedom."

We should not just dismiss a conflict. We should resolve it. A conflict usually happens between fairly close people, so if not treated properly, we can lose a close person. When we overcome a conflict, our lives can be healthy and happy. God intended peace, blessings, and good fruits for our lives. He didn't intend conflicts, fights, and hurts for us. Let us look at some guidelines to help overcome conflicts.

A Healthy Self-image Overcomes Conflicts

First, we need to have a healthy self-image. A healthy self-image in Christ can help us overcome conflicts, as many conflicts actually are generated from within. Rather than outside environments or external factors, conflicts usually start within ourselves. A true self-image in God makes our souls healthy. We become more resilient to criticisms and attacks from outside so we don't fall or get offended easily. A strong conviction of faith and self-confidence rooted in God make us resilient. Without this confidence, on the other hand, we will get hurt easily and collapse in the face of trivial issues and criticism. Therefore, the first secret to overcome conflicts is to build a healthy self-image in Christ.

Apostle Paul seemed to have many good attributes. He was from a good family background. He was academically achieved, competent, and very fruitful once he converted to Christianity. Even he had a complex or a sense of inferiority about the legitimacy of apostleship. His opponents always chased and attacked him. They monitored him closely and were aware of his weak spots. They wanted to attack his weakness to crumble him, and the weakness they found was the apostleship issue.

Jesus selected twelve apostles and kept them close. After the betrayal of Judas, Matthias took his spot, so Paul wasn't one of them. Additionally, Paul never met Jesus or learned directly under him during his three-year ministry. Where does the authority of apostles come from? It came from the fact that they heard Jesus' words from himself. Apostles took care of various matters inside and outside of church. They could lean on their authority, saying Jesus handled the matter the same say. But Paul didn't have such a direct interaction with Jesus. He didn't witness miracles firsthand, either. The opponents attacked his legitimacy as an apostle. They questioned the gospel that he taught. How could anyone not be hurt under such a scrutiny?

However, Paul proclaimed about his apostleship as follows. "Paul, an apostle—sent not from men nor by a man, but by Jesus Christ and God the Father, who raised him from the dead" (Gal 1:1). He declared that he was entitled by Jesus Christ and God. The basis for his declaration was his personal experience with the resurrected Jesus. The first qualifying condition for an apostle is to have personally met Jesus. Paul not only met Christ in person but was commissioned by him to be a witness to the gentiles. Although people did not accept his qualification, Paul remembered vividly how God met him and appointed him as an apostle. So he was able to boldly rebut them.

We cannot live healthfully if we easily get swayed by others' opinions. If we measure our lives by others' evaluations, praises, or compliments, it would be difficult. A sense of inferiority originates from comparing oneself to others. It generates negative emotions. If we subject ourselves to evaluations based on relative comparisons, we will end up living, feeling chased and unconfident. We exist because of God. As Paul confidently declared, God acknowledged and raised us up. Let us have a healthy self-image with this confession. If we firmly believe our precious value in Christ, we can live confidently regardless of how others treat us.

Some time ago I was fascinated by this title of a book that a magazine introduced. The book title was *What Life Could Mean to You*. The subtitle was *Why Do We Always Stumble in the Same Spot?* The author of this book was Alfred Adler, a renowned psychologist who is one of the three giants in the field, along with Sigmund Freud and Carl Jung. Adler also coined some psychological terms such as complex, reward (compensation) psychology, and need for recognition. His prescription for happiness was to overcome ourselves, as we were in our own way. We could either make ourselves stand tall or fall down. But he didn't provide "how" to do it. Maybe it is the limit of psychology. Many self-help books get published in the field of psychology. Generally they are about having positive or proactive attitudes. They provide some practical tips and action steps, too. Some trendy examples are "improve your self-image by looking in the mirror and kissing yourself every day," "tell yourself that you are special ten times a day," and "wear a T-shirt that says 'I'm worthy.'"

But do these really help us discover our true worth and value? These action steps tell us to do something to improve our worth. For example, we could get another degree in school, gain good working experience, get into a prestigious firm, groom our appearance, or buy a luxury brand item. But would these really enhance our value or help us realize it? I believe not.

We have to meet Jesus Christ in order to restore our true worth. There is no other way. We were sinners before we knew Jesus. But after we met Jesus, he made us anew and healed our brokenness through the power of his blood on the cross. We became new creations. We were not made by the world. We did not come into being on our own, either. We were created by

God and reborn by Christ. We became worthy because of God. Let us remember our identity in God and impress it in our minds. We can overcome any criticism and insults from the world because we have a conviction in his love. We can also boldly rebut to the world that uses wealth or appearance to measure our values. When we have a healthy self-image in Christ, we can rise above conflicts.

A Blessing Overcomes Conflicts

The second secret to overcome conflicts is to bless others. Typically people want to take revenge after they get hurt or offended. Revenge is never the right solution to resolve a conflict. Revenge begs for another revenge and can never address the root issue. So the Bible advises the opposite. We should instead bless the person who hurt us. When we bless others, we can rise above conflicts.

Paul proclaimed to the members of the Galatian church who opposed and betrayed him, "Grace and peace to you from God our Father and the Lord Jesus Christ." The word "grace" comes from "charis" in the original text which was very highly valued by the Greek. In Hebrew, it is "shalom," also very highly valued by the Jews. Paul blessed them in the best way, rather than paying back in bitterness. This is a mature attitude. Changes happen and new doors open with blessings.

They had adored and followed Paul when Paul visited them in Galatia on his first missionary journey. They took Paul's eye-related pain as their own. The same people who loved and respected Paul, turned their backs overnight. The people of Judaism overtook them after Paul left. They turned their hearts so quickly that Paul even asked how they could turn to another teaching after such a bonding.

How would one feel at such a sudden betrayal? Only those who had been betrayed would know. As for Paul, he still blessed them instead of arguing or rebuking them. An interpersonal relationship is not a bill of exact repayments. If we still bless our enemies and wrongdoers, God will pour us bigger blessings.

Paul had taught earlier, "If your enemy is hungry, feed him; if he is thirsty, give him something to drink. In doing this, you will heap burning coals on his head" (Rom 12:20). The enemy that expected a retaliation, would be baffled after receiving grace. It would be like having burning coals on his head. He would be dumbfounded at the unexpected, opposite treatment. This would germinate an internal change in him. Let us bless our wrongdoers. Our lives will be transformed. We can rise above conflicts.

Look unto Jesus

We should model after Jesus in order to overcome conflicts. Jesus Christ is the most perfect role model. Paul presented Jesus as the best role model and shared that he "gave himself for our sins to rescue us from the present evil age, according to the will of our God and Father" (Gal 1:4).

Originally there was a thick wall of conflict between God and us. Since we were sinners, we could not come before him. Since God is righteous, he had to deal with our sins. Thus our relationship with God was broken, and the wall between us was too high. No one could tear it down. Then Jesus Christ came between God and men as a mediator and redeeming sacrifice. He gave himself. Because of his sacrifice, we are saved from eternal condemnation and atoned for our sins. The word "atonement" or "ransom" is ἐξέληται ("exhelletai") in Greek, meaning "completely eliminate or get out of." Jesus Christ completely eliminated all our sins through his blood on the cross. This achieved peace between God and men, and men could receive God's blessings and eternal living.

We could be wronged by someone as we go on living. We could be misunderstood and accused when we are innocent. Consider who would be more wronged than Jesus. He was blameless without sin, yet he underwent the heaviest punishment for us. It is painful when we are betrayed by trusted ones. But consider who was more betrayed than Jesus.

Jesus came to earth for the people he saved and they abandoned Jesus. He taught, nourished, and guided his disciples for three years, but on the night of his arrest, they all left him. On the most painful and lonely night, everyone fled. Even Peter denied Jesus three times after he gallantly promised to stay by his side three times. How would Jesus have felt?

But Jesus didn't say a single word of blame or condemnation on this matter. To his last moment, he prayed for forgiveness to those who did not know what they were doing. He died, blessing those who betrayed him.

Jesus let go of all his rights and even his own life so that all men could be saved from eternal condemnation and separation from God. Because of Jesus, we can be at peace with God and receive his grace. If we were to follow Jesus, we would be able to forgive anyone. At the moment of conflicts, we should look unto Jesus.

It's never easy to forgive those who hurt you or stabbed you to leave a deadly wound. Forgiving is already hard, so blessing is even harder. Because we still have our old selves and egos in us, we gravitate towards taking revenge to get even. We cannot overcome this old ego by our own will or strength. It's impossible to practice forgiving and loving. It's only possible when our old egos die and Christ lives in us. The living Christ in us will help us rise above conflicts and share God's peace with everyone.

Some years ago, a new magazine in Japan caught people's attention. It was because of its cover. On the cover was an ordinary gray butterfly. Interestingly it turned into a colorful and eye-catching butterfly upon touching. Perhaps the designer wanted to send a message that a loving touch can transform a grim reality into a hopeful and colorful future.

The field we live our daily lives in can be pretty grim. Perhaps our homes, workplaces, or communities could be dark and depressing. We may get a glimpse of dark and depressing aspects of life in our close neighbors' lives as well. What they need is a loving touch. When we lend our hands with the love of the cross, these grey dark lives can be transformed into more beautiful and worthy lives with a fresh breath of the Holy Spirit. Let us model the love of Jesus and help our neighbors in need.

TREAT PRECIOUS THINGS WITH CARE

> But God struck down some of the inhabitants of Beth Shemesh, putting seventy[a] of them to death because they looked into the ark of the Lord. The people mourned because of the heavy blow the Lord had dealt them. And the people of Beth Shemesh asked, "Who can stand in the presence of the Lord, this holy God? To whom will the ark go up from here?" Then they sent messengers to the people of Kiriath Jearim, saying, "The Philistines have returned the ark of the Lord. Come down and take it up to your town." So the men of Kiriath Jearim came and took up the ark of the Lord. They brought it to Abinadab's house on the hill and consecrated Eleazar his son to guard the ark of the Lord. The ark remained at Kiriath Jearim a long time—twenty years in all. Then all the people of Israel turned back to the Lord. (1 Sam 6:19—7:2)

The 9/11 attack was probably the biggest disruptor among recent events in US history. This terrorist attack incident rattled entire US systems and beliefs. Not only at the national level, it permanently changed people's lives at the individual level.

In the following year (2002), a story was published in the *New York Times*. It was about an IT senior director who oversaw the computer operations of a stock trading company in Manhattan. On September 11, 2001, he was attending a seminar on 110th floor of the World Trade Center. An urgent matter came up during the seminar, so he got out of the building and headed to his office. Then an airplane hit the building. The building was in explosive flames instantly and crumbled while fire rained down. Many people who were on top of the building threw themselves into the Hudson River out of desperation. A hundred colleagues of his all died on the 110th floor. His nephew, a fireman, died in the line of duty. Sixty-seven people became victims from his town alone. As his company closed down due to the 9/11 terrorist attack, 1,800 workers lost their jobs. He became unemployed, too. He lost his job of thirty-five years overnight. It was such a big loss.

Yet he confessed that he found a silver lining even in this catastrophe. He rediscovered the value of family and warm hearts. Because he was so committed to his job for thirty-five years, he didn't really spend time with family. The moment everything he worked for disappeared, he realized that there are things more precious than making money at stocks. They were a human life and a loving family.

We tend to take for granted the precious things already in our hands. But when we lose them, we finally realize their value and learn to appreciate them.

To Treat Precious Things with Care

Israelites valued the ark of the Lord as the most precious thing, as it represented God's presence and glory. Israel actually had lost it once, then reclaimed it. It was not their work. The enemy got scared by God's mighty power and sent it back on a cart to which two cows were hitched.

So the ark of the Lord returned to Israel by itself. Interestingly, two castle towns showed very different attitudes. "God struck down some of the inhabitants of Beth Shemesh, putting seventy of them to death because they looked into the ark of the Lord" (1 Sam 6:19). The people in Beth Shemesh took the ark carelessly. They didn't treat the sacred ark with appropriate respect and casually looked into the object with curiosity. They violated instructions from God and insulted him. As a consequence, many people died, and the castle town people mourned in grief.

On the other hand, how did the people in Kiriath Jearim treat it? They took the ark to Abinadab's house on the hill and consecrated his son to guard it. They didn't neglect the ark. They paid respect to the ark and kept it holy. They took the proper care to place it in the right place. As a result, the whole castle town as well as Abinadab's house got blessed.

The ark of the Lord is a basis of blessings to all. Depending on how it was treated, one town ended up mourning, and the other town received blessings. Our lives work the same way. Although God gives us all something very valuable, some people may suffer dire consequences for mistreating it. Only those who treat it properly receive blessings. Take our family for example. Family is a precious source for blessings from God. Yet to some, family is a ground for pain and suffering. The same goes for children. To some parents, their children are like thorns that pierce their hearts for a lifetime. Those who didn't take good care of their health have no choice but to deal with illnesses. So whatever is given to us, let us deal with it wisely.

What would be most valuable in life? What precious gift did God give us? It could be people in our lives, our basis for livelihood, or a spiritual reward. Yet if we don't treat it properly, none of them can be a blessing to us. Let us now examine how we can take proper care of God's gifts.

A Heart to Cherish Our Treasure

To properly keep treasure God gave us, we need a heart to cherish and keep it well. The people of Kiriath Jearim cherished the ark of the Lord like treasure.

First, they moved it to Abinadab's house "on the hill." A house on the hill meant a holy place in Israel. It was set apart and reserved for a holy purpose. They usually built an altar on the mountain. So the most holy and historic place in Israel was Abinadab's house.

They didn't leave the ark on the streets, subject to passersby looking into and touching the holy ark. They made sure to protect it in a holy place. We have to put treasures in a treasure chest. We can protect it when we cherish it. We keep precious memories close to our hearts and cherish them. We can access when we think of them and preserve if we safeguard them in a special place.

A problem arises when we undervalue our treasure and treat it carelessly. We say a worship service is precious though sometimes we do not treat it wholeheartedly. If we act like spectators or do not respect worship by being on time, then we are not treating it properly as we should. We may also say God is precious, though he is not really on top of our priority list. Are we only saying with our lips that we love and respect God, while worship and prayer are not our highest priorities? If we are not living it, how can we say we love God?

Family is the same way. If family is precious to you, you have to put in time and effort. You have to show you care. One caveat of Korean married men is that they tend to neglect wives and children when they are young. Consequently they pay the price at later years.

Han-sook-hee Oh wrote in her book *Married? Live Together or Not?* a story of a retired physician. After he retired, he moved to a small town for seniors and opened a clinic. All his patients were elderly seniors. Typically when a man got sick, his wife would accompany him to the clinic. As he observed many cases, he noticed two types of elderly married couples.

The first type was what he called a "desperate nursing" type. A wife genuinely cared for her husband and nursed him dearly. He could tell such a wife right away as she entered his office. She would plead as if the illness were her own. "My poor husband cannot sleep a blink at night." As she emotionally presented his case, her husband would buffer by saying, "It happens to old people." If a nurse issued medicine, she would ask detailed questions, like what it is for, how to take it, etc. If a nurse had to inject a needle, she would plead to do it softly for him. Sometimes, after the couple left the clinic, only the wife would come back for one last question. Usually it's about money. "How much would it cost to do an entire body exam?" Then she would plead again that she would somehow take care of the bill, so her husband could receive the exam.

The second type is a "harassing" type. In this case, they come it with a distance from each other and also sit apart. If the husband comes out of office, frowning, then she bickers that an injection is supposed to sting a little. If the husband asks the nurse whether the medicine is okay to swallow, then the wife cuts in, saying that it won't kill anyone. She might add, "I already told you many times to quit drinking. You didn't listen and got sick like this."

The author of the book concluded as follows: "You should add savings regularly to the 'wife' piggy bank while young. It cannot be filled up all at once later in life. You should show care and love every day. It may appear small but cannot be substituted with a huge sum later on."

We should cherish precious things from the start. We should not be neglectful. To live a beautiful and fulfilling life, we need a heart to cherish our treasure.

The Will to Protect Our Treasure

We also need a will to protect. While it's important to cherish treasure, we need to protect and preserve it properly. The people of Kiriath Jearim took further precautionary steps after moving the ark to Abinadab's house. They consecrated his son, Eleazar, to guard it. To prevent damage or theft by an intruder, they set up a guard who would watch day and night.

As much as owning God's gift, protecting it with good maintenance is also important. Once it gets lost, it will be very difficult to find. While in our hands, it's best to take good care. Therefore we need a will to protect and preserve our treasure while we have it near us.

Esau painfully regretted before God. He was the elder son of Isaac. He came out earlier than his twin brother, Jacob. So by birthright, Esau was given the elder son's privilege. His big mistake was that he took it lightly. He didn't know or appreciate the true meaning of that privilege, as it wasn't on a document or visible like shiny gold. Another reason might be that since his father was alive, he had not had chance to see the effect of his birthright.

In fact, tremendous blessings of God were promised in the elder son's birthright. God gave "blessings" to Abraham at the time of making a covenant. "I will make you into a great nation, and I will bless you; I will make your name great, and you will be a blessing. I will bless those who bless you, and whoever curses you I will curse; and all peoples on earth will be blessed through you" (Gen 12:2–3).

His blessings ultimately included the coming of Messiah in the Abraham's lineage to complete God's kingdom. These amazing blessings were exclusive part of the birthright.

However, Esau failed to recognize such a precious treasure that he was entitled to. How did he handle it? He sold it for a bowl of red stew. He exchanged the holy treasure, God's promise of the eternal kingdom for stew, to satisfy his physical hunger. He learned of his mistake many years later. He tried to get it back, but it was too late. "When he desired to inherit the blessing, he was rejected, for he found no chance to repent, though he sought it with tears" (Heb 12:17).

We have to protect the blessings that God grants us. Once taken away from us, they don't return even if we try to reclaim them. Parents should protect their children and raise them well under their care. They have to protect them by praying and teaching the words of God. These days our children are exposed to evil and toxic cultures. All kinds of temptations surround them to steal and destroy. Parents must protect them with prayer.

I gave a sermon for youth teachers and parents of my church. It was on Deut 6.

One amazing fact of Israel's history is that their faith was passed down to the next generations. Israelites were in slavery for 430 years in Egypt. It probably wasn't too hard for the first generation to retain their identity. Like Jacob and Joseph, the first generation lived honoring God's words and remembered him. So even on a foreign soil, they were able to continue to live as God's people.

But it probably was a bigger challenge to keep that identity for the second generation. If we estimate 30 years to be a time span of one generation, then 430 years' time covers about 15 generations. How would it be possible to preserve and pass down the first generation's beliefs and legacy over 15 generations? It would most likely be impractical and impossible. Take Korea for example. It's common to not remember history only 3 generations ago. In Israel's case, a great leader like Moses came after 430 years. He had the identity of a Jew and a vision to leave Egypt. Joshua came to be another great leader after 430 years and played a major role in occupying the promised land. There was a secret to maintaining and inheriting the spiritual legacy from prior generations.

"Hear, O Israel: The Lord our God, the Lord is one. Love the Lord your God with all your heart and with all your soul and with all your strength. These commandments that I give you today are to be upon your hearts. Impress them on your children. Talk about them when you sit at home and when you walk along the road, when you lie down and when you get up" (Deut 6:4–7).

This passage is also called "Shema (Listen)." It's God's commandment to parents to teach their children his words. It protected Israel's spiritual identity and heritage over many years. It was not Israel who kept God's laws. God's words kept Israel. His living words protected the integrity of their beliefs and values as God's people in the toxic Egyptian culture. God protected the future of Israel.

If we wish for a bright future for our children, we have to guard them with prayer and God's words while they are with us at home. Only prayers and God's words can protect them from this stubborn and corrupt world.

The Love that Waits for Treasure

We need one more thing to treat God-given treasure to us properly. Despite our best intentions, our treasure sometimes gets damaged. When that happens, should we just give up once it's damaged? When a precious person leaves us, can we let him or her go and just forget about it? We probably will long for reconciliation through love, though the relationship may be damaged.

First we need a heart to cherish, and secondly, we need a will to protect our treasure. The last thing we need is the love to wait with patience. Israel mishandled the ark of the Lord and lost it to the Philistines. Then God was at work, and the ark returned to the land of Israel. However, it didn't reach the sanctuary and remained in the surrounding Kiriath Jearim region for twenty years. Due to this, Israel could not experience God's presence (upon the ark) for two decades. They longed for God. "It was a long time, twenty years in all, that the ark remained at Kiriath Jearim, and all the people of Israel mourned and sought after the Lord" (1 Sam 7:2). Although they lost the ark by their own fault, they still sought after the Lord, the source of all blessings.

Later, the ark was moved to a Jerusalem castle during King David's reign. On that day David danced out of joy as he had a special heart for God. The ark once again became the center of Israelites.

Let us not give up when we have lost our treasure due to our misconduct or sin. God eventually restores us if we come clean before him in prayerful waiting. He will help us find what we lost and be reconciled with broken relations. Life is full of failures. We all have failed at life in some way at some point because we didn't treat our treasures right and wasted away our precious time.

Still, God waits for us. Like the ark that eventually returned to Israel, an opportunity of recovery will visit our lives. The golden opportunity will surely transform our worthless and chaotic lives into brand new ones that will shine like precious treasure. Therefore, let us trust God and come before him. We will find what we lost. God will fill our cup. Let us come to God who will bless our lives to be worthy.

FOLLOWING JESUS

[4] Now Mesha king of Moab raised sheep, and he had to pay the king of Israel a tribute of a hundred thousand lambs and the wool of a hundred thousand rams. [5] But after Ahab died, the king of Moab rebelled against the king of Israel. [6] So at that time King Joram set out from Samaria and mobilized all Israel. [7] He also sent this message to Jehoshaphat king of Judah: "The king of Moab has rebelled against me. Will you go with me to fight against Moab?"

"I will go with you," he replied. "I am as you are, my people as your people, my horses as your horses."

[8] "By what route shall we attack?" he asked.

"Through the Desert of Edom," he answered.

[9] So the king of Israel set out with the king of Judah and the king of Edom. After a roundabout march of seven days, the army had no more water for themselves or for the animals with them.

[10] "What!" exclaimed the king of Israel. "Has the Lord called us three kings together only to deliver us into the hands of Moab?"

[11] But Jehoshaphat asked, "Is there no prophet of the Lord here, through whom we may inquire of the Lord?"

An officer of the king of Israel answered, "Elisha son of Shaphat is here. He used to pour water on the hands of Elijah."

[12] Jehoshaphat said, "The word of the Lord is with him." So the king of Israel and Jehoshaphat and the king of Edom went down to him.

[13] Elisha said to the king of Israel, "Why do you want to involve me? Go to the prophets of your father and the prophets of your mother."

"No," the king of Israel answered, "because it was the Lord who called us three kings together to deliver us into the hands of Moab."

[14] Elisha said, "As surely as the Lord Almighty lives, whom I serve, if I did not have respect for the presence of Jehoshaphat king of Judah, I would not pay any attention to you. [15] But now bring me a harpist."

While the harpist was playing, the hand of the Lord came on Elisha [16] and he said, "This is what the Lord says: I will fill this valley with pools of water. [17] For this is what the Lord says: You will see neither wind nor rain, yet this valley will be filled with water, and you, your cattle and your other animals will drink. [18] This is an easy thing in the eyes of the Lord; he will also deliver Moab into

your hands. [19] You will overthrow every fortified city and every major town. You will cut down every good tree, stop up all the springs, and ruin every good field with stones."
[20] The next morning, about the time for offering the sacrifice, there it was—water flowing from the direction of Edom! And the land was filled with water. (2 Kgs 3:4–20)

Someone knocked on his door when the genius artist Leonardo da Vinci was working on a painting. It was his neighbor, and he asked for help with a broken plumbing pipe. Da Vinci was very close to finishing what might become his next masterpiece, but he stopped his work to help his neighbor. After he got back, he just could not finish his painting. Due to the repair work, the sensitivity in his hands got dull. He tried again the next day, then the day after. But he couldn't complete the painting. The title of the painting is "Adoration of Magi," and it still remains unfinished.

There are times when things do not pan out as we wish. Unexpected obstacles appear to block our progress. They could even twist our whole lives or suffocate us as if we are trapped in a hole. Being angry at the situation won't help us. Blaming another person at fault or the environment won't help, either. What we really need is faith to find the right way. Only God opens a way when we are in need. The Bible doesn't promise us an easy life, free of tests, trials, or temptations. But it promises that God will show us a way out. Let us not fall into despair in face of hardships. Instead let us look unto the escape route that God already prepared for us.

Taking the Path God Has Prepared

It was a time of war between Israel and Moab. What started the war was the rebellion of King Mesha of Moab. King Mesha raised sheep and had to supply the king of Israel with a number of lambs along with wool of a hundred thousand rams. But after King Ahab died, the king of Moab rebelled. King Mesha is known to be an actual historic figure because an archaeological artifact was found in 1868 near the Jordan region bordering the Dead Sea. It was the Mesha gravestone with the king's name on it. Also in chapter 3 of the book of 2 Kings were recorded events related to the war. The king of Israel was called Omri, and Moab believed that they won with help of their god, Chemosh. Moab had been a subordinate country to Israel since the time of Omri and supplied goods as tribute to the northern kingdom, Israel, every year.

The annual tribute amounted to a hundred thousand lambs and wool from a hundred thousand rams. Moad had to give such a large quantity to keep peace as a subordinate. Then after Ahab died, Moab took the opportunity to rebel against Israel. It's usually more maddening if an opponent, previously regarded as weak, challenges you. King Joram of Israel reacted that way. He recruited soldiers from multiple regions of Israel. He then brought King Jehoshaphat and King Edom of the southern Israel onboard to form allied forces of three nations.

The allied forces chose to take the more difficult route. It was more common to take the route that passed through the Jordan River, heading north, in order to get to Moab. It was more comfortable for walking. However, the army took a detour around the southern part of the Dead Sea. It was more distant and challenging. But the enemy's defense line was probably more relaxed on that route. Hannibal of Carthage also had used such a strategy when invading Rome. No one expected an invasion from the Alps side. King Joram prepared meticulously. He formed a mighty military force and had a strong strategy of attack. All he had to do now was to execute the attack.

However, a problem arose. As the allied forces were taking a long detour for seven days, they ran out of water. The horses they took with them also could not drink. According to theologians Keil and Robinson, this happened in the Ashi valley, which originally was next to a river in proximity. We can guess that they probably weren't too concerned about water due to the river. But in reality, the river had dried up after continued drought in that region. They were in a big trouble. Neither the soldiers nor the horses had water to drink. There was no water in the valley, and if they got out of the valley, the Moab army would strike them.

If we were ever in this kind of situation in our lives, what breakthrough would we expect? No human methods will be useful. We have to turn to God for a breakthrough.

Look for the Right Guide

We need to find the right guide to find a breakthrough. When we run into a dead end, we need a guide to find the right way. King Jehoshaphat looked for a prophet because he wanted to ask God. From his standpoint, the war broke out by King Joram of the north, and he was only recruited to join the war at a big risk. His kingdom could get harmed if the northern Kingdom of Israel lost. He proactively looked for a way to survive. "Is there a prophet who can ask God?"

Perhaps southern Israel had good faith. They seemed to seek God's counsel through a prophet when facing a problem. That was appropriate for God's people. One of the officials mentioned Elisha. He was also the pupil of Elijah and his successor. The southern kingdom of Israel probably heard of Elijah's high reputation, as he was a legendary prophet in his time. He probably thought highly of Elijah's pupil.

In fact, Elisha received a multiple of Elijah's spiritual inspiration by request. He was in a deep communion with God and could probably read God's will well. When we deal with urgent problems, we should not frantically find anyone. We have to go to a godly person, someone who can guide in his direction.

Men tend to wrestle alone rather than seek counsel when they have problems. They show such a tendency when they get lost while driving. As for women, they tend to ask for directions right away. This helps them get back on the right track fast. On the other hand, men are more stubborn and just keep on going without a sense of direction, until they finally run out of gas. This is not advisable. We have to stop and ask for directions. We have to find the right guide who can help us.

Who would be this guide when we are lost? He listens to anything we say and answers to any silly question without judging us. It is Jesus Christ. Jesus is our best guide. He was God and man like us at the same time. He is not unapproachable high up there with no understanding of what we go through on earth.

Jesus became like us. He passed through life. He felt hunger and pain. He also was rejected, betrayed, hurt, abandoned, and beat up. He knows our reality so well. While he knew our pain, he was also blameless without sin. So Jesus alone is "the way, the truth, and the life" (John 14:6).

When you feel burdened with problems in life, come to God and ask him. Then he will be your guide. Do not deal with it alone. I encourage you to come before Jesus. He will provide the best solution with kindness. He is the architect of our life path. No one else knows it better.

Receive God's Answer

Secondly, we need to receive God's words. After we meet the right guide, we need to receive God's answer through him. King Jehoshaphat firmly believed that Elisha could give God's answer to him. So the three kings from Israel, Judah, and Edom together went to see Elisha.

Those who give sermons or share God's words are probably envious of Elisha in two aspects. First, Elisha was the person they thought of when in crisis. That meant he was a precious person a nation leaned on. It was an affirmation of his greatness. As parents, we want to be the ones our children think of when they are in trouble. We should not be the ones they put aside, thinking we cannot help them. As for Elisha, people thought of him when they faced a hardship. Next, Elisha was equipped with God's words. Everyone acknowledged him as God's messenger. We do not need to be envious of rich people or handsome people. Let us envy those who are empowered by God's words. They know the truth and knowing the truth is same as having all the answers to life.

At the Harvest Crusade in Philadelphia, in September of 2013, Pastor Greg Laurie said the following in his message. A small kid was learning the Ten Commandments at Sunday School. He said he understood all the rest, except the seventh. What is the seventh commandment? It is "Do not commit adultery." It was above his age. So he came home and said to his father that the seventh commandment was too hard to understand. Then his father asked what it was. The kid responded, "Do not commit agriculture." His father smiled and said, "Do not plant your seed into someone else's field." How accurate and age-appropriate his reply was.

We need wisdom to understand God's words. If we can correctly answer in God's words at any questions thrown at us, it would be an extraordinary ability and aptitude. Elisha fit into that category. When three kings came to him for advice, Elisha delivered God's message. "This is what the Lord says: I will fill this valley with pools of water. For this is what the Lord says: You will see neither wind nor rain, yet this valley will be filled with water, and you, your cattle and your other animals will drink" (2 Kgs 3:16–17).

God's first instruction through Elisha was "to dig many waterways in the valley." The valley had already dried up and the bottom was exposed. If any water was seen, it would have made more sense to dig waterways, as more water could be collected. But what use would it be to dig further into the completely dry land? There were no signs of rain or storm. It would not be easy to waste labor and efforts on something that had no chance of happening. God's messages often seem to be contrary to the usual logic or good common sense. God does not always ask us to do things that are easily understandable or agreeable. He is outside our boundaries some-times. However, God told them, "this valley will be filled with water, and you, your cattle and your other animals will drink."

God said it because he could take responsibility. He intended to do it, so he let them know. He was not bluffing or daring them to do it in vain. He said that if they dug more waterways, the valley would be filled with water. Notice that God's words are on another level than a man's words. What God speaks is already reality in a sense. As he speaks, it will be done in actual life. If he says, "Let there be land," then land will come into being. Likewise, if he says, "Let there be the sky," then the sky will be created. His words are powerful.

Elisha kindly added supplementary explanation for the kings with little faith. "This is an easy thing in the eyes of the Lord; he will also deliver Moab into your hands" (2 Kgs 3:18). God went beyond and even promised their victory in war. It was the ultimate wish of Israel. They chose to take the long detour and endured the thirst to execute a winning strategy against Moab. All they had to do now was to dig waterways. This is the power of God's words. The solutions to our problems in life are already in his words.

It is really amazing that all solutions to all problems humans can face in life are provided in God's words. Therefore, if we listen to God's voice and obey, we can experience miracles as God permits. We don't have to look far to find a breakthrough in our lives. It's near us and it's in his words. When we are troubled, we should hold onto his words more.

In our disciple training, having a daily Q.T. (Quiet Time, daily medita-tion of the Bible) is a vital requirement. It could feel like homework. Dur-ing the 3–4 months of training, we check homework, so participants force themselves through the Q.T. Some graduate from Q.T. as they complete the training curriculum. Some repeat the cycle of 3–4 months of Q.T. followed with 8 months of no Q.T. When we do daily Q.T. preferably in the early morning, God's words can be impressed on our hearts as we go through the day and they protect us. They become our guide of the day. Let us honor God's words every morning and live each day victoriously.

Offer a proper sacrifice

The last step to find a breakthrough is to offer a proper sacrifice. After the three kings followed Elijah's message from God and made waterways, water from Edom flew into the valley and filled it in the morning. God's words were actualized. In general, a rainfall is needed to generate water. Alternatively, we can dig a well until the underground water is found. The water they received was not from either source. God's works are truly mysterious. What solution did he provide when Israelites met the Red Sea in Exodus? His solution came from under the sea of the impossible. His solution was not far away. It was within reach, yet beyond our comprehension. Water could not possibly be generated anywhere in that dried up valley, but God made water flow into the valley from the direction of Edom. The valley was filled with water, enough for all men and animals. God worked his miracle again.

There was another wondrous work of God. The water in the valley appeared to be red blood to the Moabites. It was the reflection of the rising sun. The Moab army believed that it was human blood from the quarrels among the three kings. They were misled by the illusion and went on to plunder. The visual illusion came from God, but the misinterpretation came from human foolishness. They added their own imagination. The allied forces must have gone in fight against one another the previous night, and all had died in battle. Off guard, they came out to pillage the battleground. The allied forces of Israel easily took the Moab army under control and ended the war.

What an amazing turn of events. How did they happen? The mysterious illusion happened "the next morning, about the time for offering the sacrifice." Here the meaning of "sacrifice" would be closer to a morning worship than grains. God's people gave offerings morning and evening. Water began to flow about the time for offering. God prepared water as well as a winning strategy. The time for the miracle was the time of the morning offering.

An offering service is a worship to God. It means giving thanks and praise. "Through Jesus, therefore, let us continually offer to God a sacrifice of praise—the fruit of lips that openly profess his name" (Heb 13:15). Apostle Paul said that God is pleased with our sanctified bodies as an offering. "Offer your bodies as a living sacrifice, holy and pleasing to God—this is your true and proper worship" (Rom 12:1).

Miracles happen when we acknowledge God and give ourselves to him. When we open our lips to praise God, living water will burst out. Freely available to those who are thirsty or in pain, living water will flow. He will turn the tide so we can win the battle.

Our secret to victory is this. We cannot win with our own strength. No matter how great and massive our ability, skills, or wealth may be, we cannot win on the battlefield of life. We cannot untangle the knots. Only when we trust in God fully and worship him with praise will God open the door, make miracles happen, and lead us to victory.

King Jehoshaphat of Judah took a priceless lesson with him home. The secret to winning a war was not in military power. It was worshiping and praising God. Applying this valuable lesson to a later war that broke out between the army of Moab and Ammon and southern Judah, he placed singing priests at the forefront before the troops. What strategy was this? A common sense tells us that at the forefront, the archers and the soldiers good at hand combats should lead the way. However, as the singing priests began to praise God, the Lord made the enemy lose. God starts working at the hour of our praises and prayers. That is also the hour when he makes our enemies fall.

We may face countless problems that we cannot handle with our own resources. Some are unexpected, and some pull us down deeper like a swamp as we try to wrestle them. Are you hurting and groaning in pain? Let us not try to find solutions elsewhere. God has already prepared a breakthrough. Let us come to the Lord, listen to him, and follow his instructions. If we praise him and pray, God will surely give us a way out. I pray that we all find a breakthrough and come out victorious.

REFORM THAT CHANGES THE NATURE

[23]Then Jehu and Jehonadab son of Rekab went into the temple of Baal. Jehu said to the servants of Baal, "Look around and see that no one who serves the Lord is here with you—only servants of Baal." [24] So they went in to make sacrifices and burnt offerings. Now Jehu had posted eighty men outside with this warning: "If one of you lets any of the men I am placing in your hands escape, it will be your life for his life."
[25] As soon as Jehu had finished making the burnt offering, he ordered the guards and officers: "Go in and kill them; let no one escape." So they cut them down with the sword. The guards and officers threw the bodies out and then entered the inner shrine of the temple of Baal. [26] They brought the sacred stone out of the temple of Baal and burned it. [27] They demolished the sacred stone

of Baal and tore down the temple of Baal, and people have used it for a latrine to this day. [28] So Jehu destroyed Baal worship in Israel. [29] However, he did not turn away from the sins of Jeroboam son of Nebat, which he had caused Israel to commit—the worship of the golden calves at Bethel and Dan. [30] The Lord said to Jehu, "Because you have done well in accomplishing what is right in my eyes and have done to the house of Ahab all I had in mind to do, your descendants will sit on the throne of Israel to the fourth generation." [31] Yet Jehu was not careful to keep the law of the Lord, the God of Israel, with all his heart. He did not turn away from the sins of Jeroboam, which he had caused Israel to commit. (2 Kgs 10:23–31)

Let me share a story of someone who was known as the "legendary student at Seoul National University." Seoul National University (SNU) is the top ranking, most prestigious, and most coveted university in South Korea. He scored a perfect score on the standardized entrance exams and got into SNU, majoring in business management. We call such a kid "Um-chin-ah," meaning an all-star kid who is academically achieved and gets into good schools and companies. He had once sent a letter to Profession Dong-sung Cho who taught business management at SNU while he was a third-year high school student. He introduced himself as a high school student in the graduating year and asked the professor of his opinion about choosing business management as his major, if he wanted to bring reforms to the corrupt society and unethical business practices. This would be analogous to a baseball hitter forewarning about the direction in which he would send a ball then making a home run in that foretold direction. This student became well-known as a legend at school and private tutoring places. He was at the pinnacle in that world, as he got into a top university with a top score.

However, he was not satisfied. He graduated college and entered law school. Then, out of desire to get a more perfect score, he broke into a professor's office to illegally obtain a copy of an upcoming exam. He got caught on site. He was hiding in a cabinet when the security guards came. Before bringing on any reforms to the society, he got kicked out of school, and his reputation was forever stained. He became the legend of the cabinet.

The toughest battle is the one with ourselves. It might be easier to change systems and structures that are visible and outside of ourselves. We can approach them objectively and make improvements. However, internal transformations within us are never easy. They require remodeling our internal selves and sanctifying ourselves to become God's people.

David is a main example. He could not control his inner self and fell into temptation. He had many admirable strengths and extraordinary achievements. After he won many battles, he remained humble. After he suffered for many years being chased, he didn't commit treason. He managed to survive, even acting like a crazy man. But he failed at an inner test, lust. Not many can win internal battles with themselves. We have egos that only we know of, while the whole world may be fooled. The egos could stay hidden for a long time, but our twisted and unhealthy egos may still be there. Our lives can become whole only after we break and change our inner selves.

After Failing at Reform

In the northern kingdom of Israel, Jehu came to power. He was the most extreme reformer in the history of Israel. He shot King Joram and had his body thrown on the field that belonged to Naboth the Jezreelite. It was revenge for the blood of Naboth and his sons by Joram's father, Ahab. Jehu also struck down Jezebel, an evil follower of Baal, and had Jezreel dogs devour her flesh. Then he also slaughtered seventy sons of the house of Ahab. He killed the king of Judah, Ahaziah, for siding with the northern kingdom and his forty brothers.

Jehu didn't stop here. He called an assembly in honor of Baal, to gather all the prophets, servants, and priests of Baal. They crowded into the temple of Baal in Samaria, which was the capital of Israel. The temple was erected by Ahab at the time of his wedding with Jezebel. How detestable it was to have the temple of Baal right in the center of God's country. With Jehonadab son of Rekab, Jehu killed them all. They demolished the sacred stone of Baal and used it for a latrine. Jehu executed unprecedented reforms.

However, there remained one thing that Jehu could not reform. He destroyed Baal worship in Israel but left behind the golden calves at Bethel and Dan. The golden calves were idols with a long history, erected by Jeroboam son of Nebat. After the people of Israel left Egypt, they had come to the Sinai Desert. Moses departed to Mount Sinai to receive the Ten Commandments, and the people of Israel were camped below. As Moses took time in coming down from the mountain, the people asked Aaron to make them gods. Aaron collected all the gold and created a golden calf, saying, "These are your gods, Israel, who brought you up out of Egypt" (Exod 32:4). So the worship of the golden calf is the root of the sin of idolatry in the history of Israel. Although Jehu reformed and destroyed everything that was used to worship Baal, he did not uproot the golden calf. Golden calf worship probably continued in his heart as well. His reform stopped short of removing the very root of idolatry.

In a way, Jehu's reform changed the clothes of the people from Baal to the golden calf. This would not be a truly complete reform. If we have enough power in politics, we can probably change systems and structures in the society. These are visible, external changes. Typically the first thing Korean politicians work on is some type of reform once they rise to power. Public servants usually stay low-key in their early years, just to survive. Once in power, they all execute reforms, only with different groups or systems. The governments that initiate change are not part of the reforms. So there has not been a case where the leaders in the government admitted their own faults and made improvements where needed. This would be the inherent contradiction in the politics of the world.

The same contradiction exists at church, too. The reforms at church also tend to be directed towards others, not at themselves. Sometimes we hear a campaign slogan, "Make it right." Upon closer inspection, we may find that the intent behind the slogan is actually "Change it like I say." There is a self-centered motive, and that is a quite dangerous paradigm.

A true reform changes the nature of something that is reformed. It doesn't change it from outside in. Rather, the change begins from within. We need to examine our own standings and see if we can start a reform from ourselves. Jehu accomplished external reforms, but failed at his own internal reform. Let us visit the reasons why Jehu failed internally.

Straighten the Motive for Reform

The first reason was his motive. His motivation was to flaunt and show himself off. It was not truly for God. We need to examine our true motive. If it is to life up God, not ourselves, then things will progress in the right direction.

Jehu could initiate reforms because he met Jehonadab, son of Rekab. The Rekab (Rechab) clan is also called Kenites. Jethro, Moses' father-in-law, was from this clan. Since they were nomads, they moved around and raised herds. So they didn't need to settle down in one spot and get along with its powerful faction. They were able to serve God purely. Jehonadab was the right person to help spearhead the reforms that destroyed Baal. Jehonadab joined Jehu for this reason. His dream was to eliminate Baal, purify Israel, unite the South and the North, and ultimately restore its status as the holy land. He didn't mean to share the power with Jehu under a new government. Jehonadab's motive was pure.

On the other hand, what was Jehu like? "Come with me and see my zeal for the Lord" (2 Kgs 10:16). He meant that he got something to show. From this verse, we can read his self-centered and achievement-oriented mindset. Let us not be mistaken. We don't want to dismiss or not acknowledge accomplishments and the fruitful works for God. We need incentives to some degree, to assign tasks well and see them come through to the end. But the most important thing would be our motive, not the actual accomplishment. So we need to clarify who a mission is meant to glorify. Wrongful motives point in wrong directions. Even if the fruits of our works may be great and praiseworthy, wrongful underlying motives nullify all our efforts and achievements.

Apostle Paul knew this and went a great length to re-examine his own motives about missionary work. "I eagerly expect and hope that I will in no way be ashamed, but will have sufficient courage so that now as always Christ will be exalted in my body, whether by life or by death. For to me, to live is Christ and to die is gain" (Phil 1:20–21). The desire of his heart was not about whether he lives or dies. His true wish was to exalt only Jesus Christ. He confessed that he's not so concerned about his living or dying, as long as Christ is exalted. "For to me, to live is Christ and to die is gain."

Are we running with a pure desire to glorify Jesus Christ? Can we join Paul in confessing that "to live is Christ and to die is gain"? This was Paul's secret of how he was able to keep running for a crown of faith, despite all the persecutions. What is our motive? What's our underlying motive for serving church? If we are doing it for reputation, applause, or recognition, we are not going in the right direction. Jesus Christ should be our only motive.

I was invited as guest speaker to a seminar for ministers a few years ago. Most of the attendees were young pastors who just had started on their pastoral journeys. Naturally their top interest seemed to be how to grow a church. The contents of the seminar also focused on many successful examples of church growth. These were stories of a very small church that grew astronomically over only a few years.

Then it was my turn to speak. I felt that my message was a bit out of place but brought up a story of Pastor Kyung-jik Han that I read in a magazine, *Monthly Pastoring*. After he retired, he received the following interview question: "Pastor Han, what was your secret to success as pastor?" He didn't respond right away. He took some moments in silence. Then finally he opened his mouth and replied, "It is not my credit, so your question baffled me for a moment. And we can only tell whether it was a success or not, when we stand before God. It seems premature to talk about success or its secret now." What a precious and humble attitude of Pastor Han.

In fact, he was the lead pastor of the biggest church in South Korea during his tenure. Tens of thousands of people attended. It would be more common to hear some strategies that worked and some bragging upon such a question. However, Pastor Han didn't frame his ministry in terms of success or non-success. In his answer, he meant that ministry is God's work and a pastor is not the right person to receive praise. This is a confession from someone who truly emptied himself. Let us not take credit for what God has done. Whatever we do, let us have a pure motive for a true reform.

Straighten up our Beliefs

The second reason to Jehu's failure was his wrong beliefs. We care about our values and beliefs deeply. So we need to examine the root of our values. Jehu accomplished external reforms, yet failed at internal reforms because he didn't let go of the golden calf, a detestable sin of idolatry.

I don't mean to say that Jehu served himself, not minding God. He accomplished a lot for God as well. He dismantled the statue of Baal and killed all the followers of Baal. He set the right tone for serving God. However, he left the golden calves at Bethel and Dan untouched. It was because they were in Jehu's heart.

The golden calves occupied his mind and heart, where God should have been. We can take the golden calves as what we value the most. In our hearts are our own versions of golden calves. If we value them more than God, they are our idols. Some examples are love for materials, fame, recognition, and pride. We all have our golden calves. Let us let go of them so God can reign in us.

Our spirits don't change because we are not serving God in our hearts. When God is in sovereign control of our spirits, transformations surely will happen. But golden calves occupying our hearts obstruct such changes. Thus we have to let go of our golden calves.

In the book of Job, it is written, "assign your nuggets to the dust, your gold of Ophir to the rocks in the ravines" (Job 22:24). Gold of Ophir was regarded as the best at that time. If we release and throw away our golden calves, then God can become our foremost treasure and best gold. Let us rid ourselves of our golden calves that we held onto for so long and bragged about. Let God reign us. If we pray to him, he will listen and fulfill us. He will open our ways to the future and tear down closed walls and doors. Whatever we work at, God will help and bless our journey.

This is the true secret to victory. Our golden calves cannot take responsibility of our lives and rescue us from crises. They cannot cure our terminal illnesses. They cannot restore peace to dysfunctional families. Only God can. He is the almighty. When he takes control in our driver's seat, true recovery can begin. Good fruits that will please God begin to appear. Let us let go of our golden calves and watch what God does to renew our lives.

Make a Spiritual Decision

The last reason for Jehu's failure was his problematic spiritual decision. Having the right motive and beliefs is not sufficient. For a true internal reform, we need to make a decision before God. God can transform us and pour new blessings unto us.

Jehu's reform stopped at the external level because he didn't "wholeheartedly" keep God's laws. He kept them, but not wholeheartedly. Many Christians try to follow God's words, receive discipleship training, and live a life pleasing to God to some degree. Jehu did, too. He probably went to worship services every Sunday. But the issue was, he didn't do it with all of his heart. "Wholeheartedness" means giving all of our heart undividedly. Let us lay down our own thoughts and focus only on God with all of our heart.

People have their egos that have developed and stayed with them for a long time. It would not be easy to break that ego. It's not easy to throw away old habits overnight.

A minister in Chicago dreamt of an ideal pasture where white and black people got along well. So he started a worship service for everyone regardless of skin color. He changed and customized the order of service, design of his church, structure of ministries as well as its congregation. Although there were some challenges and issues, the adult members generally adapted well. We know that adults have acquired their social skills over time, so they know how to behave in different social situations. Even when they don't totally agree, they can go along with the flow. However, children were different. They were transparent about their likes and dislikes and expressed that honestly.

On a Sunday, children were riding a bus. A teacher noticed that they were sitting in two groups. The white kids were on one side, and the black kids were on the other. The teacher thought it was a teaching moment. She asked the white kids. "What color is your skin?" They all said that it's white. Then the teacher emphasized. "No, if you look closer, it's a little dark. It sometimes has spots. Your skin color is not all white. It's grey. You see?" She wanted their confirmation by asking again. "What color is your skin?" They reluctantly replied, "It's grey."

Then she asked the black kids the same question .They all said that it's black. She explained again that if they looked closer, it's not as dark as black. It's mixed with white sometimes. She said to them that their skin was grey. She asked for confirmation. "What color is your skin?" All the kids responded in unison, "It's grey." The teacher got off the bus, feeling relieved.

The next Sunday they got on the bus again and saw an interesting scene. A kid was controlling the traffic inside the bus, saying "Hey, the lighter greys, come to this side. The darker greys, go to that side."

Education, though needed, does not transform people. Training is needed, but it doesn't change people, either. We have to deal with the roots in our heart. Until the root is treated, a true transformation will not happen. Only the Holy Spirit can touch our egos and inspire them to change. Our ability, determination, or will cannot. The Holy Spirit has to work in us. So we have to open our hearts and wholeheartedly seek God's grace. Then the power of the Holy Spirit will touch our spirits. Changes will begin. Our inner selves will begin to become like Jesus Christ. This is sanctification.

Our egos are problematic. They were formed over many years, so there are some parts that we are not even aware of. We have to break our false egos, as they obstruct the passage to God's blessings and relationship with us. We may have unconfessed sins in our hearts. Even if men may not know, God knows.

Let us not hide. Instead let us give our burden to God. Jesus died on the cross because we couldn't save ourselves. Our lives are futile, and our ability is limited. Let us bring our sins and hurts to the cross. If we have bitter roots of deep emotional wounds and hurts, we need to bring them all before Jesus. The hardened wall of our wounded hearts can be torn down and healed by the Lord. Let us all surrender our arrogance, selfishness, and pride to God. Ask him to become our Lord. Let us confess to the Holy Spirit and ask to be renewed.

TOWARD A LIFE OF VITALITY

> Now Moses was tending the flock of Jethro his father-in-law, the priest of Midian, and he led the flock to the far side of the wilderness and came to Horeb, the mountain of God. There the angel of the Lord appeared to him in flames of fire from within a bush. Moses saw that though the bush was on fire it did not burn up. So Moses thought, "I will go over and see this strange sight—why the bush does not burn up." When the Lord saw that he had gone over to look, God called to him from within the bush, "Moses! Moses!" And Moses said, "Here I am." (Exod 3:1–4)

Boris Becker was the "prince of tennis" in the 1980s. He was a German tennis player who became the youngest ever winner of the gentlemen's singles Wimbledon, when he was only seventeen years old in 1985. He was a young, handsome, rich, and popular number one tennis star. However, he attempted suicide two times in his life. In his autobiography *The Player*, he confessed that he was dependent on popularity and acceptance from people and he became completely fatigued at life.

When people fall into helplessness or low energy, it's usually due to a lack of passion rather than a hostile environment. If the fire in their hearts dies because they cannot find their calling and purpose, no great success or wealth can sustain the empty life. Christians should beware of lifelessness and loss of energy as well. Even Christians can become inactive and low in energy, although the Holy Spirit and the power of gospel is with them. If Christians became helpless, who would then transform the world, shining the light in the darkness and spreading hope? Christians have to fight and overcome being unenergetic and unmotivated. They have to live a life of vitality. Are we living daily with thrills and challenges? Or are we living like we are being dragged into another day with no motivation and calling? How can we break the vicious pattern of helplessness and live an abundant life?

Toward the Fire of Life

Moses was a good example of someone who boldly broke out of a lifeless living to pursue God's vision. Commonly Moses' life is introduced in three parts, with each part spanning about forty years. Moody explained Moses' three parts of life as follows. In the first forty years he came to realize who he was. In the next forty years he realized that he was a "nobody." Then in the last forty years he realized that God was everything.

In the first forty years he learned that he was a Hebrew and God's child. Baby Moses grew up with his mother's milk because his mother disguised herself as his babysitter. In the ancient days a babysitter typically took care of a baby for five years. What would Moses' mother have taught Moses in his first five years? She probably taught him that they were Jews, the only people of God. The early education from mother probably established his identity as God's child before the regular Egyptian education and customs influenced him for the next thirty-five years. We can say that mother's teaching dominated over the later institutional education. We probably cannot overemphasize the importance of mother's teaching at home.

In the next forty years, Moses learned that he was a "nobody." His situation helped him realize this, as he spent forty long years as a shepherd in the Midian wilderness. It was a result of escaping Egypt after killing a man out of rage. This humbling step was necessary for the next step where he came to commit his whole life to God who was everything. "I am nothing" is the pre-requisite of "God is everything." It may be worth it to look closer into how this shift of perspective occurs.

He was eighty years old at the end of the second forty-year period. The time of ambitious youth was behind him, and a meditative time for a mature man was beginning. This period came after his days in the palace as prince, followed by the days in the wilderness. Moses went out to the field in the morning, looked after the sheep, and came home in the evening. He repeated the next day. He lived this simple life for forty years. During this routine period, he probably lost his vision, passion, and motivation. It was almost like he was barely surviving each day, filling his time with mundane routines. We can ask an important question at this point in his life. What made him transform into a great leader that guided the Israelites out of Egypt?

"There the angel of the Lord appeared to him in flames of fire from within a bush. Moses saw that through the bush was on fire it did not burn up" (Exod 3:2). This happened on the mountain of God, Horeb. He saw that a bush was on fire yet did not burn up. The fire kept on burning, not consuming the bush. The moment he experienced God's fire, Moses' life began to change.

What does a bush mean? It's a small, unassuming tree in the Palestine region. In the wilderness dried up bushes are scattered. They look unimpressive and useless. A bush may symbolize two things. First is Israel's people. At the time, the Israelites were slaves of Egypt and were dried up like the bushes of the wilderness. Secondly, the bush symbolizes Moses himself. He had been dried up in the desert over forty years. All his passion was gone.

A new chapter in history could begin, when God's fire came upon the hopeless bush. It was a fire God had in store for us. People of the world have their fires, commonly called ambitions. Success is possible when there is a burning ambition. A strong motivation can help get ahead of others.

Steve Jobs gave a speech at a graduation ceremony at Stanford University. Many people regard this highly, saying it was very motivational. He said, "stay hungry" and "stay foolish." It's remarkable that with these few words, he could rekindle young people's hearts. But let us remember that the fire Steve Jobs rekindled is not the eternal fire. It undeniably will die out eventually. The fires of this world may temporarily excite and inspire us, but they certainly have limits. Time will prove that they all turn into ashes.

However, God's fire is the living fire. It can revive a dying soul. It's a fire of miracles. It will burn down all impossibilities and bring about God's works. All of us need to receive God's fire of hope to see his vision and go forward toward his vision. Most of all, this fire is eternal. The fires of the world are temporary, but God's fire keeps burning by eternal anointing.

Depending on which fire we occupy ourselves with, the fruits of our lives will be different. The fires of the world may tempt us with its splendor and glory but will eventually die out in ashes. On the other hand, God's fire can transform our lives to be great. We all need his fire. Let us look into the ways in which we can receive God's fire to overcome lifelessness and get up toward his vision.

Go to Mount Horeb

If we want to recover from persistent low energy and motivation, we need to go to Mount Horeb. That's where God is present. Without seeing him, we cannot see his fire, either. To summarize the second forty years of his life,

Moses was shepherding the herd of Jethro, his father-in-law and a priest of Midian. All he did during that time was working each day as a shepherd.

One day he drove the herd toward the west of the wilderness and arrived at Mount Horeb. A Korean translation used the expression "west of the wilderness," which meant the farthest end of the wilderness. The job of shepherds is to drive the sheep around and feed them. If possible, they probably stayed close to home. For some reason, Moses went further out that day, reaching to the west end of the wilderness.

So he went and there was a magnificent mountain. It was Mount Horeb. "Horeb" means desolate and barren. God's place was desolate and barren. In the Bible, there is another mountain of God called Sinai. They both could refer to the same place. Some theologians interpret that Horeb refers to the entire mountain while Sinai refers to a specific point in that mountainous area. Another theologian interprets that southern Judah called the mountain Sinai, while northern Israel called it Horeb. A similar case would be Mount Baek-du in North Korea, which is called Mount Jang-baek in China. Anyway, this mountain was the place of God's presence.

When Moses arrived at Mount Horeb, no one was to be seen. Horeb was not a place people frequented. It was not a civilized place. It was a quiet and barren field of nothingness only with the sound of wind. In this place Moses met God. This meeting forever changed his course of life and rejuvenated his life.

To meet God one on one in person would be an amazing blessing. No one else was around. Only God and Moses were present without any disruption or interference. In that special hour, even the barren field of nothingness turned into the most holy place. We all need such an encounter. One unique part of Jesus' daily routine was that he woke up at dawn and went to a quiet place to pray. Jesus prayed at dawn every day. It was his daily habit. At that hour, the place of prayer was the wilderness, in which no one was. Jesus went out to the wilderness and observed a daily holy hour without any disruptions. It was just between God and him. The one-on-one with God was the main engine of Jesus' life and the core of his ministry.

Our lives need Mount Horeb. It's a place where we commune with God deeply. In modern days people are too busy to meet God. This is actually a serious issue. If our lives are too busy to make time for God, they probably need adjustment. Keeping busy doesn't equate to doing fruitful work. Overbearing ourselves with excessive activities could cause burnout. Then we can no longer continue. When we encounter God, he renews us.

He refreshes and replenishes us. Time with God provides us with his authority and power.

Elijah was one of the most powerful prophets in the Bible. He did fruitful works for the glory of God. He went into King Ahab's palace and declared war against all the followers of Baal. He singlehandedly kept fighting for more than three years. He won the battle against 850 prophets who followed Baal on Mount Carmel. He was a powerful servant of God who prayed and made it rain after a three-and-a-half year drought period. Elijah was such an accomplished prophet, yet he fell apart surprisingly by something seemingly trivial. After he was threatened by Queen Jezebel, he fell into despair, sat under a broom bush, and pleaded to the Lord to just let him die. We can attribute his sudden fall to one reason. He was burned out. As he focused his energy on ministries and various works, he no longer maintained a single focus on God.

We need our works and ministries. It is our reality to take charge of many assignments and tasks. But unless we are careful, we might lose our sight of God, distracted by other pertinent priorities. If our tasks and activities take our focus off God, not only will our fruits be right, but also we cannot stand straight in faith. Our deep communion with God itself fuels us.

Later in his day Moses guided the people of Israel, and he went back to Mount Horeb. He spent forty days and nights alone with God. As a consequence, his face was radiant when he came down from the mountain. His face shined, unlike any other lights of this world, because he had spoken with the Lord. People couldn't look directly in his face due to the brightness received from God's authority and power.

We all need such a power. We long to become such a godly being of God's presence that the evil and dark forces do not dare to touch. His breath revives us. Let us prioritize God first and come to him. The time with God should be a time of joy. Then our spirit will revive and our lives will be recovered.

Experience the Fire

We also would need to experience God's fire to recover from spiritual lifelessness. After we encounter God on Mount Horeb, we need to see his fire in person. Moses saw that though the bush was on fire it did not burn up. So Moses thought, "I will go over and see this strange sight—why the bush does not burn up" (Exod 3:2–3). So Moses didn't dismiss it when he noticed a strange phenomenon. He went over to see what it was about.

The "strange sight" represents a spiritual scene that accompanies the coming of the Holy Spirit. We also remember how a violent wind came from heaven and filled the whole house, along with what seemed to be tongues of fire that rested on each disciple on the day of Pentecost. We should not think of the Holy Spirit's presence at an abstract or conceptual level. As written in the book of Acts, the event was actual and real. It was a very specific event that we could even touch and feel. The 120 God-fearing Jews at Mark's house, as well as those believers at Jerusalem, marveled at the strange phenomenon. Unbelievable works happen where the Holy Spirit comes. Strange sights unfold. But if we are not there to see them, it will be of no use. Therefore we have to go over, see the fire of God, and make the experience our own.

Moses went the distance to turn around and look at the "strange sight." Some may run away or avoid unusual sights, but Moses reacted differently. He took steps to be closer to it. This is the work of faith. Instead of denying or withdrawing from the presence of the Holy Spirit, he approached a history in making with an open heart. So he was able to encounter the Holy Spirit and witness God's fire. The coming of the Holy Spirit on Pentecost is not a one-time, expired event of the past.

Many scholars say that the Pentecost event was a historic occurrence that happened once. They say that it was a single occurrence just like the Calvary event. I agree that the Pentecost event was real in history. But I must add that it is not completely over because the works of the Holy Spirit are ongoing. The same Holy Spirit who came to Mark's house two thousand years ago is still at work at present. He is one and the same for eternity. The Holy Spirit that shares the character of God is present continuously and timelessly. He is at work as of this moment as well. If we believe and come before the fire of God with open hearts, the wondrous works of the Holy Spirit will unfold before our eyes.

Moody started his ministry with a great fervor in Chicago, but in the early days the ministry didn't take off so well. Then one day, he noticed two sisters who were praying with eyes closed in the first row. They were praying with eyes closed during the entire worship service. One was Sarah Cooke, and the other was Mrs. Hawxhurst. After the service, Moody asked them, "What were you two doing during the service?" They answered, "We prayed that the Holy Spirit come upon you with a strong force." After hearing their answer, Moody asked them to keep praying for him. As God answered their prayer, Moody received the Holy Spirit, and he grew from being a small church pastor to being a great nationwide evangelical messenger in the US and Europe. We can call this Moody's Pentecost event.

We all need our own Pentecost events. Our lives can be transformed if we encounter the Holy Spirit the way the Holy Spirit came upon the 120 believers in Mark's attic two thousand years ago. It's not the power of the world or the environment. We need to let the power of the Holy Spirit lead and transform our lives. I sincerely wish that we all experience the fire of the Lord. I also wish that our churches be transformed by the powerful presence of the Holy Spirit. Let our churches be God's instruments that witness God's power in the last days.

Obey

We need to experience obeying God, in order to change our unmotivated and un-energized lives. Although it is of vital importance to meet God and commune with him deeply, it alone cannot help us bear good fruits. We need more than receiving the fire of the Spirit and rekindled passion. We need one more, and it is obedience. When we obey to God's calling, his power will be unleashed.

God saw Moses approaching the bush and called him, "Moses, Moses." He already knew his name and called him personally. The creator of the universe was calling a person's name. It was a wonderful moment. God knows each and every one of us by our name, too. There is a reason when God calls us. It's because he has something to say. He has a vision to fulfill through us. Therefore, if we hear God calling our names, we should respond properly, "Here I am."

Our answer with "here I am" is an important step. In truth, it's only half of a complete answer. If we stop here, we cannot carry out God's will. The second half would be "Send me" (Isa 6:8). So when God calls us, we should give our complete answer with obedience: "Here I am. Send me."

Moses did not immediately obey God after he first heard his calling. He found excuses. He said that he was not much. He was too small to take on God's big works. So he advised God to find another person better suited for the role. He made excuses multiple times and tried to bail out. Then finally he obeyed: "Send me to Pharaoh's palace." So Moses went before the most powerful king of Egypt, only holding a staff.

The footsteps in obedience are the first gateway to a miracle. Moses did not have anything. He only had a staff. Nonetheless, when he obeyed God, the staff delivered a miracle to open the Red Sea. If our lives are unmotivated and barren, it's not because we don't have access to power. Without God's presence, our lives are inherently lifeless. Problems seem impossible and enemies appear invincible. But if God's power fills us and renews us with strength and courage, we can withstand any difficulty in any situation and become God's workers.

Are our lives in good health? Are they staying sitting down in lack of energy and motivation?

We all need Jesus Christ when we cannot get up by ourselves in our own strength and abilities. We need the Holy Spirit, the living God in us. When the Holy Spirit empowers us, the dying fire of vision can be rekindled in our cold and barren spirit. We can boldly run towards God's dream for us at the higher level. When we are completely burned out, incapacitated, or exhausted, let us not despair. Instead, let us come before God. Jesus will renew and revive us.

Closing Words

A Dawn Arrives with Jesus

The following story is from Charles E. Cowman's *Mountain Trailways for Youth*. There was a young man who led a disorderly life. But after getting to know Jesus, he cleaned up his act and started a new job in a street light maintenance crew. His job was to turn on lights at night and turn them off at dawn. One day a few old acquaintances that enjoyed drinking came to him and asked, "How's life treating you after you followed Jesus?" The young man explained his new job and responded as follows: "Every dawn I look back after turning off street lights. It's just like looking at my dark past. But when I look ahead at a long array of lights that are still on, I see hope. It's like looking at my future." His old friends responded in a mocking tone: "You fool, where will you go then, after the last light goes out?" The young man smiled and said, "Don't worry. After the last light goes out, a new dawn will have already started to break. Then we don't need street lights anymore."

A nighttime can fall on anyone's life. As the dawn light brightens, we don't need street lights any more. The sun will smother all the darkness and illuminate ahead. This is the essence of a Christian life as well. We cannot turn over the course of a darkening life with our own power. We cannot subdue the night in all our futile attempts. However, things will be different when Jesus comes into our lives. He is the light and the sun of righteousness. He brings a new dawn into our lives. It's not because he provides solutions to our questions. Rather, our questions themselves will disintegrate. All the answers are already found in him. Zacharias confessed with a following song: "because of the tender mercy of our God, by which the rising sun will come to us from heaven to shine on those living in darkness and in the shadow of death, to guide our feet into the path of peace" (Luke 1:78–79). Yes, indeed. The dawn arrives with Jesus Christ. Therefore, let us not be afraid of the night. Let us not fear our despair and confusion-ridden realities. In his presence, all will be illuminated and renewed.

The Gospel books record incidents where apostles faced a storm in the sea. Sea storms were quite unpredictable in Galilee. In front of an oncoming gigantic wave, no one would be able to guarantee the fate of a boat. Being in the middle of the sea in the darkest hour of night would only make matters worse. Who could possibly beat such a big storm of despair? The apostles' efforts to row and steer the boat would not be sufficient. But when Jesus came into the picture, the roaring storm stopped. The turbulence calmed down and quiet peace was restored. Mark recorded that the time was around 4 o'clock at night. The 4 o'clock here means the dawn hour of 3–4 am until before a sunrise. With the coming of Jesus, the night storm ended and a dawn arrived. This kind of experience was not exclusive to the apostles.

The moment when a woman of Samaria met Jesus at the well, her night of shame and inadequacy ended, and a new dawn began in her life. Consider the Canaanite mother of a demon-possessed daughter, the woman who was dragged out in the public for committing adultery, people who suffered from leprosy, the beggar who had been lame from birth for 38 years, and the blind beggar at the streets of Jerusalem. As soon as they came in contact with Jesus, a new dawn came upon their lives. This would apply to our own lives as well. Let us not despair or give up in the face of grim realities. A dawn will begin when we meet Jesus.

A life can be compared to a long journey at sea. At times, we may face gigantic waves or pitch-black hopelessness in various situations. However, we can be assured that when the true light, Jesus Christ is with us, we don't need to fear. He will guide a way. In him are life, healing, and true hope. No matter what the circumstances are, we can get back up with him alongside us.

Let me share a story of Dave Dravecky, a professional baseball player. He was a left-handed pitcher who played for seven years for the San Diego Padres and San Francisco Giants. Unfortunately, he got cancer in 1988 and had to undergo surgery on his left arm. This was a critical surgery to a professional athlete. People thought that he would not be able to come back. But against all odds, he not only came back to play after the surgery, but also threw eight innings to a team victory. But five days after, his arm was fractured and had to be amputated. Most people might have fallen into despair and even given up on life, yet he was different. After his retirement as an athlete, he founded a mission organization called Outreach of Hope and embarked on an evangelical ministry. He also wrote a book which was published in 1990. The book title was *Come Back*. In his book, he challenges us all in the following way: "If you can't come back with your own feet, come back with Jesus Christ."

Let me share this same challenge with you all. *When we can't get up on our own, get back up with Jesus Christ.* With him, we can look in a new direction and proceed towards a new vision, a vision that is completely worthy of our lifelong commitments. A new morning of abundant blessings awaits us all.

www.ingramcontent.com/pod-product-compliance
Lightning Source LLC
Chambersburg PA
CBHW060344100426
42812CB00003B/1123